OECD Reviews of Health Systems: Latvia 2016

OECD
BETTER POLICIES FOR BETTER LIVES

This work is published under the responsibility of the Secretary-General of the OECD. The opinions expressed and arguments employed herein do not necessarily reflect the official views of OECD member countries.

This document and any map included herein are without prejudice to the status of or sovereignty over any territory, to the delimitation of international frontiers and boundaries and to the name of any territory, city or area.

Please cite this publication as:
OECD (2016), *OECD Reviews of Health Systems: Latvia 2016*, OECD Publishing, Paris.
http://dx.doi.org/10.1787/9789264262782-en

ISBN 978-92-64-26276-8 (print)
ISBN 978-92-64-26278-2 (PDF)

Series: OECD Reviews of Health Systems
ISSN 1990-1429 (print)
ISSN 1990-1410 (online)

The statistical data for Israel are supplied by and under the responsibility of the relevant Israeli authorities. The use of such data by the OECD is without prejudice to the status of the Golan Heights, East Jerusalem and Israeli settlements in the West Bank under the terms of international law.

Photo credits: Cover © Tomi/PhotoLink/Photodisc/Getty Images, © Tomi/PhotoLink/Photodisc/Getty Images.

Corrigenda to OECD publications may be found on line at: *www.oecd.org/about/publishing/corrigenda.htm*.

Foreword

Latvia's health system broadly delivers effective and efficient care to the population within a context of significantly fewer resources – and higher health care needs – compared to most OECD countries. Latvia has successfully consolidated its hospital sector and strengthened primary care. Average length of stay in hospital fell by almost 15% between 2005 and 2013, and GPs are now required to follow up on patients who called for emergency medical assistance but were not hospitalised. OECD health systems could learn much from these reforms as well as longer-standing institutions, such as Latvia's *feldshers* (physician assistants).

Latvia nevertheless faces important challenges to maintain and improve the performance of its health system. Up to one in five Latvians report forgoing health care because of the cost; waiting times for key diagnostic and treatment services (such as cancer care) can be long; and inclusion of key treatments in the publicly-funded benefits basket does not always reflect latest best practice. Critically, the health system lags behind many OECD countries in the degree to which data are used to systematically measure, compare and improve the performance of services, especially at more granular provider or local levels. This review aims to support Latvia to continue its reforms of the health system, informed by international best practices. Chapter 1 describes Latvia's health care needs, recent reforms to the health system and its current configuration. Chapter 2 assesses performance of the Latvian health system, with a particular focus on accessibility, quality, efficiency and sustainability, and makes recommendations for strengthening these dimensions of performance. Chapter 3 focuses on primary care, again making recommendations for strengthening this sector.

This health system review consists of a report prepared by the OECD Secretariat to support the review of Latvia undertaken by the OECD Health Committee as part of the process for Latvia's accession to the OECD [see the Roadmap for the Accession of Latvia to the OECD Convention [C(2013)122/FINAL]. Latvia acceded to the OECD Convention and became an OECD Member on 1 July 2016.

ACKNOWLEDGEMENTS

The lead author of this *Health System Review* is Ian Forde. The other authors of this report are Rie Fujisawa, Emily Hewlett and Carol Nader. The authors wish to thank Gaetan Lafortune, Francesca Colombo, Mark Pearson and Stefano Scarpetta from the OECD Directorate of Employment, Labour and Social Affairs for their comments and suggestions. Thanks also go to Marlène Mohier for her editorial input and to Duniya Dedyn, Susannah Nash and Judy Zinnemann for their logistical assistance.

The completion of this report would not have been possible without the generous support of Latvian authorities. This report has benefited from the expertise and material received from many health officials, health professionals, patient groups and other health experts that the OECD review team met during a mission to Latvia in December 2014. These included officials and representatives of the Department of Public Health, Intersectoral Cooperation Division, Department of Health Care, Division of Primary Care, Department of Pharmaceuticals, Department of EU Funds, Environmental Health Division and the Division of Strategic Planning at the Ministry of Health; the National Health Service; the Emergency Medical Service; the State Agency for Medicines; the Central Statistical Bureau; the Centre for Disease Prevention and Control; the Health Inspectorate; the Latvian Medical Association; the Latvian Health Care Employers Association; the Latvian Hospital Associations; the Latvian Family Doctors Association; the Latvian Rural Family Doctors Association; the Latvian Nursing Association; the Pharmacists' Society of Latvia; the Latvian Insurers Association; the Sustento Umbrella Body for Disability Organisations in Latvia; the Patients' Ombudsman Office; the Latvian Association of Regional and Local Governments; and staff from Valmiera Regional Hospital, Valmiera Municipality and Dr Harasimjuka's primary care practice in Valmiera; Professor Dr. Ģirts Briģis of Riga Stradins University and Professor Andrejs Ērglis of the University of Latvia.

The review team is especially thankful to Minister Guntis Belēvičs and his officials at the Ministry of Health, especially Solvita Zvidriņa, Egita Pole, Daina Mūrmane-Umbraško, Agnese Raboviča, Kristīne Kļaviņa and Ludis Pauliņš, for their support for this review and their help with setting up the visit of OECD officials to Latvia. This report has benefited from the comments of the Latvian authorities and experts who reviewed earlier drafts.

Table of contents

Tables

Figures

Acronyms and abbreviations

ACSQHC	Australian Commission on Safety and Quality in Health Care
ALOS	Average length of stay
AMI	Acute myocardial infarction
CBT	Cognitive behavioural therapy
CDPC	Centre for Disease Prevention and Control
CME	Continuing medical education
COPD	Chronic obstructive pulmonary disease
CTO	Community Treatment Order
CVD	Cardiovascular disease
DDD	Defined daily dose
DRG	Diagnosis-related group
EU	European Union
Eur	Euros
GDP	Gross domestic product
GP	General practitioner
HCQI	Health Care Quality Indicators
HI	Health Inspectorate
HPV	Human papilloma virus
LMA	Latvian Medical Association
LNA	Latvian Nursing Association
LTC	Long-term care
MoH	Ministry of Health
MoW	Ministry of Welfare
MRI	Magnetic resonance imaging
NHS	National Health System
OOH	Out-of-hours
OOP	Out-of-pocket
PCI	Percutaneous coronary intervention

PPP	Purchasing power parity
SEMS	State emergency medical service
SUSTENTO	Latvian Umbrella Body for Disability Organisations
USD	US dollar
WHO	World Health Organization
YLD	Years lost to disability

Executive summary

Latvia's health system broadly delivers effective and efficient care to the population within a context of significantly fewer resources – and higher health care needs – compared to most OECD countries. The health system's response to the effects of the 2008 global financial crisis was agile and well-targeted: EU funds were channelled towards transforming small hospitals into outpatient facilities and developing the infrastructure of the bigger hospitals. Latvia achieved a decrease of nearly 15% in average hospital length of stay, from 9.6 days in 2005 to 8.3 days in 2013. The number of outpatient visits increased by 19% between 2005 and 2010. Recent reforms in primary care are also notable: a compulsory pay-for-performance scheme was introduced in 2013; general practitioners (GPs) receive payments to detect first and second-stage cancer in registered patients to promote early diagnosis; and Latvia introduced an alert system to inform GPs by email about patients who called for emergency medical assistance but were not hospitalised. OECD health systems could learn much from these reforms as well as longer-standing institutions, such as Latvia's *feldshers*, or physician assistants.

Latvia nevertheless faces important challenges to maintain and improve the performance of its health system. Up to one in five Latvians report foregoing health care because of the cost; waiting times for key diagnostic and treatment services (such as cancer care) can be long; and inclusion of key treatments in the publicly-funded benefits basket does not always reflect latest best practice. Critically, the Latvian health system lags behind many OECD countries in the degree to which data are used to systematically measure, compare and improve the performance of services, especially at more granular provider or local levels.

To meet the nation's health challenges effectively and sustainably, the Latvian health system must improve access to care, by considering the re-introduction of cost-sharing exemptions for vulnerable and low-income groups, and deliver preventive care more effectively. It must also better use data, by developing key performance indicators across the system, and renew the strategic vision for the health care system, in particular through further consolidation of the hospital sector, through transformation of the National Health Service (NHS) into a strategic purchaser and planner, and through development of a comprehensive plan for the health care workforce.

Key recommendations include creating a data-driven health care system (by developing key performance indicators on access, quality, efficiency and sustainability; and by benchmarking provider-level performance measures); improving access to care (in particular by reducing out-of-pocket health care spending); improving the quality of care (through wider collection of data on quality and outcomes, and implementation of a national system to learn from adverse events); delivering preventive care more effectively (through better use of nurses in GP practices, and better using pharmacists for preventive care); and, increasing health spending per capita to a level closer to the OECD average through a targeted, incremental increase in spending.

Assessment and recommendations

In the context of tough epidemiological, financial and organisational challenges, Latvia's health system is delivering broadly effective and efficient care to the population. Since independence in 1991, the Latvian health system has experienced multiple cycles of far-reaching reorganisation and unanticipated external shocks. An initial shift toward decentralisation (away from the inherited Soviet-style centralised health system) created 119 municipalities. Within the health system, these were meant to manage service delivery and drive reforms at the local level. Many, however, had a population of less than 2 000. Later thinking concluded that a decentralised system was not appropriate for a small country with a population of around 2 million, and Latvia shifted back to more centralised governance. The most recent and most profound external shock, however, was a near-halving of the health budget, following the 2008 global financial crisis. Faced with these challenges, there is nevertheless much to praise in Latvia's health system, and a range of innovative aspects that OECD health systems could learn from.

The Latvian population benefits from universal health care insurance, delivered in a single-payer system financed through general taxation. Within the national health system (NHS), there is a purchaser–provider split and both public and private providers can compete for NHS contracts. In recent years, Latvia has strengthened the role of the Ministry of Health and other national bodies in health system governance. The central government's current strategy focuses on the reorganisation of care for four priority diseases (oncology, cardiovascular disease, neonatal care and mental health, based on their high burden of disease in the country) and emphasises the development of quality assurance mechanisms, and e-health, human resource planning (particularly in rural areas) and health promotion. Municipalities are also responsible for health promotion and prevention activities, and they are supported by the Ministry and the Centre for Disease Prevention and Control (CDPC) to develop information campaigns and other activities. Municipalities also organise long-term care services and, in some cases, subsidise patients' transportation costs. Quality assurance mechanisms focus on assuring safety, and the health information infrastructure has been developed and expanded.

Following two decades of impressive economic growth, in which Latvia narrowed the income gap relative to OECD economies, the impact of the global financial crisis in Latvia in 2008-09 was very harsh, with Latvia experiencing one of the worst output losses in the world. Far-reaching fiscal consolidation measures were introduced, including in the health sector. Health care is funded with a very low rate of public investment compared to OECD health systems, equivalent to just 3.2% of GDP (2013 figures). Substantial out-of-pocket spending brings total national expenditure on health to 5.3% of GDP (equivalent to 1 217 USD PPP per person per year). Simultaneously, the stability of the Latvian health system is jeopardised by an equally daunting and rapidly evolving set of intrinsic challenges. The most important of these is Latvia's rapidly ageing and declining population: the emigration of working-age adults has seen the population drop by more than a tenth between 2009 and the present day.

Latvia has responded to budget cuts with a range of efficiency measures. Some sophisticated and dynamic payment systems have been developed, especially for primary care, which are backed by a national price tariff and global budgets. A national master plan, developed with the World Bank, reduced the number of hospital beds from 8.8 to 5.8 per 1 000 population between 2000 and 2013 (OECD, 2015a; OECD, 2015e). Quality has not been sidelined, as evidenced by a recently introduced performance management framework for primary care doctors. A similar system for hospitals will soon follow. Patient groups report being well involved in policy making and several intersectoral memoranda of co-operation have been agreed – including with industry – on key public health issues. Medical education is also excellent, with Latvian medical schools having maintained their reputation as among the best in the ex-Soviet world.

These significant instances of progress and innovation in the Latvian health system must be set against some serious causes for concern, including persistent problems around unmet need, shortcomings in care quality, and significant challenges to sustainability. Access has deteriorated on several fronts: up to one in five Latvians report foregoing health care because of the cost, waiting times for key diagnostic and treatment services (such as cancer care) can be long, and reimbursement of drugs and procedures is not always consistent with latest clinical evidence or guidelines. Preventive health care suffered particularly badly as a result of the budget cuts and is poorly delivered. E-health and IT solutions are in development but so far unevenly used. More broadly, the Latvian health system lags behind OECD countries in the degree to which available data are used to systematically measure, compare and improve the performance of health services, especially at more granular provider or local levels. There has also been a lapse in the strategic vision driving health sector reform. Further rationalisation of the hospital sector is needed, in parallel with development of better networks and pathways of care, yet there is no clear strategy in place to achieve this.

To meet the nation's health challenges effectively and sustainably, the Latvian health system must now:

- renew the strategic vision for how health services are to be delivered, in particular through further consolidation of the hospital sector, through transformation of the NHS into a strategic purchaser and planner, and through the development of a comprehensive plan for the health workforce;
- make health care a data-driven system, by developing key performance indicators across the system, moving to open publication and benchmarking, and by developing provider-level performance measures;
- improve access to care, by strengthening the gatekeeper role of GPs and considering the re-introduction of cost-sharing exemptions for vulnerable and low-income groups;
- improve the quality of care, by going beyond minimum standards, considering voluntary accreditation, developing clearer and better applied guidelines, and better using data (including disease registers and adverse event registers) to understand shortcomings in care quality;
- deliver preventive care more effectively, for example through better use of nurses in GP practices, and better using pharmacists for preventive care.

Sustainable policy making is a real challenge in Latvia, at all levels of the health system. At a government level, unstable financing, a high turnover of Ministers, and the under-exploitation of data on health system performance mean that policies are too often scattergun and short term. To finance the health system, Latvia relies not just on a high out-of-pocket contribution from patients, but also on European Union contributions. This means that policy makers are unsure of the budget that they will have to work with in the years to come, and it is difficult for payers and providers to develop longer-term strategies. To some extent, the significant financial challenges that Latvia has faced in recent years has accelerated the pace of change and had a positive impact, for instance speeding up reforms to the hospital sector. In other respects though, financial pressures have meant that focus is dragged back to the short term. As in most OECD countries, long-term investments in population health have suffered.

Two underpinning structural features, both admittedly complex, will need to be addressed to enable the health system to deliver its goals. First, greater stability in the governance of the health system would be desirable. Latvia has had a high turnover of 11 ministers of Health in the past 12 years, inevitably limiting the extent to which mid- to longer-term strategic reforms can be implemented. Second, the health system will unquestionably need greater public funding in future years. Even compared to other former Soviet economies, the Latvian system is under-resourced. Estonia and Lithuania, for example, spend approximately 1% of GDP more on health. Whilst also limiting the feasibility of longer-term reform, underfunding is also harming Latvians' health today, as evidenced by the numbers foregoing health care and late treatment of diseases as a result. If national health and wellbeing is a priority for Latvia, more public money will need to be directed to its health system.

Latvia's health care needs and health care system

The health of the Latvian population remains relatively poor, with low life expectancy, increasing prevalence of non-communicable disease, high mortality rates, cardiovascular diseases, cancer, traffic accidents and suicides. Population ageing is progressing more slowly than in many OECD countries, but is nonetheless complicating the disease-burden, and adding pressure to the health system. At the same time, prevalence of communicable diseases such as HIV remains high.

Latvia's demographic and socioeconomic context

The population of Latvia peaked at almost 2.7 million around 1990 but has dramatically dropped by more than 20% to reach less than 2 million in 2014. The working-age population has declined rapidly due to migration to other European countries, which was accelerated after independence in 1991 and the global financial crisis in 2008. Since 2000, Latvia has lost approximately 14% of the working-age population (Hazans, 2012). Between 2008 and 2013, on average 30 000 people left every year, particularly the young and relatively well-educated (OECD, 2015f; OECD, 2013b). Health professionals such as doctors and nurses are no exception to this pattern. Population decline and a decreasing number of people of working age are expected to continue over the next decades because of low fertility rates and the continuing trend of emigration.

Although those aged over 65 represented 18.6% of the Latvian population in 2013, above the OECD average of 15.6%, the Latvian population is not ageing as quickly as many OECD populations. In 2050, the share of the elderly aged 65 and over is expected to reach 22.8% in Latvia while the OECD average is expected to be 27.1%. Nonetheless, the ageing population, exacerbated by higher levels of emigration amongst working-age Latvians, will increase health system pressures in the years to come. The dependency ratio of the elderly aged 65 and over to the working-age population aged between 20 and 64 is growing more slowly than the OECD average but will be 41% in 2050.

Box 0.1. Key features and institutions of the Latvian health system

The Latvian health system is, like most OECD systems, broadly split across primary care, community and outpatient, and secondary hospital and specialist care. Primary care physicians, dental care providers and pharmacies are predominately private. Most hospitals are owned by municipalities, although tertiary hospitals and specialised hospitals are owned by the central government.

The **hospital sector** has been reformed significantly since 2004, as part of a move to consolidate hospitals and specialist services and to shift from inpatient care to outpatient care and medical care at home. The number of hospitals contracted by the NHS declined from 72 in 2008 to 39 in 2012 (Taube et al., 2015). There were 5.8 hospital beds per 1 000 population in 2013.

Primary care services are paid by a mix of payment methods including capitation, fee-for-service and pay-for-performance. **In-patient care** used to be paid through fee-for-service up to a specific upper limit but after several years of a transitional period with a quasi-diagnosis-related group (DRG) system, the introduction of a DRG system began in 2015. **Specialist out-patient care** is paid mainly by a flat rate determined for diagnostic groups such as acute diseases, chronic diseases and prevention, and fee-for-service payments.

Coverage and service tariffs are set by the NHS. The coverage of products and services reimbursed by the NHS is based on health technology assessment, which evaluates affordability and cost efficiency for pharmaceutical goods, but not for medical devices and procedures.

The NHS started to reimburse medical care at home in 2009. Medical care at home has been developed for patients with chronic disease and movement difficulty, for instance, after surgery, for stroke patients and palliative care patients. Family support, however, continues to play a significant role in caring for patients at home, and support for carers (such as respite periods or financial allowances) are less developed than in some OECD health systems. There is also a system providing social care at home, which comes under the responsibility of the Ministry of Welfare.

At the central level, the Parliament, the Cabinet of Ministers and the Ministry of Health are the key players in making decisions on the Latvian health system. The Parliament approves the budget for the NHS, which has the responsibility of purchasing health services, and the Health Subcommittee within the Social and Employment Committee of the Parliament reviews all health-related matters raised by its members and other stakeholders. The Parliament and the Cabinet of Ministers issue main normative acts and regulations for the health system.

The **Ministry of Health** is responsible for national health policies and regulations and the overall organisation and functioning of health system and supervises the implementation of specific measures related to priority policy areas. The Ministry also regulates public health activities and co-ordinates activities undertaken at the local levels in the areas of health promotion and disease prevention.

Municipalities at the decentralised level have a limited role but are responsible for assuring access to health care services to their population, implementing health promotion and prevention activities and organising and providing long-term care services. The NHS takes charge of administering the funding and purchasing function of the health system at the central level based on contracts with providers. Other main tasks include setting annual quotas for health care services that it finances in order to control the public outlays each year.

Box 0.1. Key features and institutions of the Latvian health system *(cont.)*

The **Health Inspectorate** (HI) is responsible for assuring quality of care. HI evaluates NHS providers and health professionals, checking compliance with national regulations.

The **Centre for Disease Prevention and Control** (CDPC), under the Ministry of Health, is the national public health institution responsible for collecting, analysing and reporting health information, managing disease registries, organising population surveys on health behaviour, epidemiological surveillance of communicable diseases, implementing public health promotion and prevention activities and monitoring disease outbreaks and public health programmes.

The **State Emergency Medical Service** (SEMS), under the supervision of the Ministry of Health, runs emergency care throughout the country.

The **State Agency for Medicine**, under the supervision of the Ministry of Health, takes charge of assuring the safety and clinical effectiveness of pharmaceutical products and medical equipment based on national and international regulations.

The health status of the Latvian population is still relatively poor

Life expectancy at birth in Latvia remains lower than OECD countries at 73.9 years, compared with an OECD average of 80.5 years in 2013. Life expectancy at age 65 is also much lower than the OECD average, at 18.6 years for females and 13.7 for males in Latvia, compared to 21.1 and 17.8 OECD averages, respectively. Overall, the mortality rate among men is 1.9 times greater than the rate among women. More specifically, mortality for men across all age groups is 6.9 times higher than women for suicide, 3.2 times higher for transport accident, 2.1 times higher for cancer, 1.8 times higher for ischemic heart diseases and 1.3 times higher for stroke. These gender differences can be explained partly by the greater prevalence of risk factors and disease incidence among men in Latvia. For example, cancer incidence is about 60% higher for men than women in Latvia while the gender gap is much lower at less than 10% in the United Kingdom, Denmark and Iceland (OECD, 2015a).

Shorter life expectancy in Latvia compared with OECD countries is explained by high mortality rates from several causes of death. The mortality rate from ischemic heart disease and stroke is three times higher than the OECD average (357 per 100 000 population compared with 117, and 200 per 100 000 population compared with 66, respectively in 2013). The mortality rate is also high for cancer (245 per 100 000 population compared with 206). Leading causes of cancer mortality are prostate cancer, lung cancer, bowel cancer, stomach cancer and bladder cancer for men, and breast cancer, bowel cancer, corpus uteri cancer, cervical cancer and ovary cancer for women (IARC, 2015). Moreover, the suicide rate and the mortality rate due to transport accidents are both higher than the OECD average, at 20 per 100 000 population compared with 12, and at 10 per 100 000 population compared with 7, respectively.

In terms of trends in mortality, the picture is mixed. For cardiovascular diseases, Latvia generally followed the same declining trend as OECD countries in the 2000s and has also experienced a slight increase in recent years as seen in OECD countries. With regards to cancer, the mortality rate has increased in Latvia since 2000, although death rates from all types of cancer among men and women have declined slowly in OECD countries during the same period. In Latvia, mortality rates from colorectal cancer, prostate cancer and cervical cancer have been increasing over the past decade. Suicide rates also decreased steadily across OECD countries in the same period, but this has not been the case in Latvia. However, infant mortality has reduced rapidly in Latvia in recent years, although the rate is still higher than the OECD average.

Latvia also needs to tackle the spread of some infectious diseases. The incidence of HIV is highest after Estonia in Europe at 16.6 per 100 000 population in 2012, and incidence of AIDS is much higher than any OECD country at 6.8 per 100 000 population, compared to an OECD average of 1.4. The number of newly-reported cases of AIDS has continued to increase in recent years while OECD countries have managed to decrease the incidence since the mid-1990s. Incidence rates of hepatitis B (for which the principal modes of transmission are the same as for HIV/AIDS are also high, with more than ten cases per 100 000 population. While this is a decline from about 40 cases per 100 000 in 2003, it is still high compared with the OECD average of two. Over the past decade, however, effective vaccination against hepatitis B among children aged 1 has led to considerable reduction of incidence in the adult population and almost elimination among children.

Self-reported health status in Latvia is poor. International comparisons of self-reported data on health status are often difficult to compare because they can be affected by social and cultural factors. In Latvia, the proportion of people reporting good and very good health status rose from 35% in 2005 to 45% in 2013. However, this is still much lower than the EU average of 67%. The proportion of Latvians reporting bad or very bad health declined from 22% in 2005 to 17% in 2013. While this is an improvement, it is considerably higher than the EU average of 10% (Eurostat, 2015). Self-reported long-standing illness or health problem and limitation in usual activities are also higher than many European countries. For example, the share of low-income population with self-perceived longstanding illness is much higher in Latvia at 44% than the European average of 33% and the share among the high-income group is 22% in Latvia, also higher than the European average of 18% (Eurostat, 2015). Differences in these rates between high and low-income groups illustrate that Latvia has high health inequality, compared to many European countries.

The prevalence of adverse risk factors is high and – of great concern – becoming worse

Smoking in Latvia is common, particularly among adult men and, contrary to most OECD countries, it is increasing (OECD, 2015a). The smoking rate in Latvia is 34.3%, almost double the OECD average of 19.7% in 2013. The gender gap is large compared with most OECD countries, and more than one in two adult men smoke every day while less than one in five adult women are daily smokers in Latvia. Between 2000 and 2013, OECD countries on average reduced the rate of daily smoking in adults by 6% while in Latvia it increased by over 1%. However, significant changes have been reached regarding smoking prevalence among youth as well as second-hand smoking prevalence in workplaces – both have decreased.

Latvian adults on average consumed 10.2 litres of alcohol per capita in 2012, an increase from 7.1 in 2000. In contrast, OECD countries on average demonstrated a decreasing trend from 9.5 in 2000 to 8.8 in 2013 (OECD, 2015a). The prevalence of obesity is also higher in Latvia at 23.6% of adults, compared to the OECD average of 19% (OECD, 2015a). Although many OECD countries have a higher share of obesity among men, Latvia does not follow this trend. CDPC figures suggest the rate is much higher among women at 25%, compared with 16% among men.

Health system spending and resources are unusually low in Latvia

Latvia spends 5.3% of GDP on health care (2013 figures, equivalent to USD PPP 1 217 per person per year), lower than the OECD average of 8.9% and USD PPP 3 453. This is partly because public funding is low in Latvia, accounting for 3.2% of GDP, much lower than the OECD average of 6.5% in 2013. Among OECD countries, only Mexico spends as little as Latvia, and Chile, Turkey and Korea spend less than 4% of GDP on health through public financing.

Growth in health spending in Latvia has been modest compared to overall economic growth. Real GDP growth in Latvia averaged about 9% in 2002-07, then contracted sharply by 3.6%, 14.3% and 3.6% between 2008 and 2010, finally picking up again at around 3% annual growth until the recent slowdown. Prior to the global financial crisis, between 2005 and 2009, health spending in Latvia increased by 3% per year, slower than the OECD average of 3.4% annual growth. Between 2009 and 2013, Latvian health spending growth was no different to the OECD average, at 0.6% per year.

Shortages of some professional groups are anticipated. There are 3.1 practising doctors per 1 000 population, close to the OECD average of 3.2, but many doctors are retiring in coming decades. The average age of Latvian GPs is 54. More than two-thirds of practising GPs are aged 50 and over, and more than a quarter are aged 60 and over (CDPC, 2014).

The number of practising nurses is of even greater concern. Nurse numbers in Latvia are low at 4.9 per 1 000 population, compared with the OECD average of 9.1. This also translates into a low nurse:physician ratio of 1.5, compared to the OECD average of 2.8. The age of nurses and other supporting professionals is also increasing, making it challenging to secure their future supply.

One notable feature of Latvia's health care workforce, which may go some way to relieving physician and nurse shortages, is the physician assistant or *feldsher.* These individuals, who are trained in emergency and outpatient care for diagnosis and prescribing, have a role somewhere between that of doctors and nurses. They fill some of the resource gap, particularly in rural areas, and offer an interesting model for OECD health systems to consider. Employing a second nurse or physician assistant became mandatory in 2014 for practices with more than 1 800 registered patients (or 800 patients under 18 years old). As of 2013, there were 1 869 physician assistants in the country. In addition, in areas where access to health care is more challenging, local municipalities have established physician assistant units. To open such a unit, the region must be without a registered GP practice; or the distance from the unit to the nearest GP practice is more than ten kilometres; or the area the unit serves has no fewer than 500 residents. There were 96 physician assistant practices in operation at the end of 2013, with an average of 4.4 patient consultations per day..

Latvia's doctors and nurses are generally considered well-trained and highly competent. As such, they sometimes seek employment elsewhere in Europe, such as in Germany, Norway and the United Kingdom. In particular, the demand for specialised nurses, such as surgical nurses and intensive care nurses, is particularly high in Europe, leading to a relatively high expatriation rate of 5% of the workforce annually (compared with the OECD average of 2.8% and the European average of 4.9%). Additionally, some nursing graduates do not choose a nursing career, due to difficult working conditions, and seek employment in other sectors within Latvia. Although many returned to nursing during the crisis (as it offered more stable employment compared to the private sector), on average about

150 nurses a year choose to discontinue nursing work, significantly offsetting the 200 to 350 nurses that are trained each year.

Access to pharmaceuticals is relatively limited. Per capita spending on pharmaceuticals is USD PPP 306 in Latvia, much lower than the OECD average of USD PPP 515. However, the share of out-of-pocket payment for pharmaceuticals is high, accounting for 18% of current health expenditure, compared with the OECD average of 7%. This suggests access to pharmaceuticals can be challenging in the country, particularly among low-income groups. Data on pharmaceutical consumption and sales are limited in Latvia but the only available data for international comparisons show that sales of antibacterials for systemic use measured in defined daily dose (DDD) are about 35% lower than the OECD average.

Latvia has been strengthening its health system information infrastructure in recent years. With the introduction of the e-health system in 2016, the availability and use of health information is expected to increase as the system will record health services delivered, tests and their results, costs and prescription information for each patient by using unique patient identifiers. Provider coverage is initially limited but the system is envisaged to cover all providers eventually. It is intended that the information systems currently used by different providers will be integrated into a single national system. This should allow, for example, health care providers to issue e-prescription so that patients can purchase medications in any pharmacy in the country. A consolidated national data infrastructure should also enable providers to monitor medication safety, when multiple drugs are prescribed, and avoid duplicate diagnostic tests by different providers. It is also expected to facilitate care co-ordination among multiple providers, for instance by informing GPs of patients discharged from hospital. Patients will be able to access some elements of their health record as well.

Latvia reports a fairly good selection of indicators as part of the OECD's Health Data collection, facilitating benchmarking against OECD countries. Latvia reports several OECD quality indicators, including avoidable admissions for asthma and chronic obstructive pulmonary disease (COPD) and diabetes, cancer screening and survival, admission-based mortality for acute myocardial infarction (AMI) and stroke, suicide following hospitalisation for a psychiatric disorder, and excess mortality for bipolar and schizophrenia. A first step in terms of improving the availability of information on quality in Latvia will be to broaden the indicators that Latvia systematically collects on quality of care, to include reporting on congestive heart failure hospital admission, more detailed prescribing data (e.g. diabetic individuals with at least one prescription of cholesterol-lowering medication in the past year), surgical complications, obstetric trauma, and patient experience indicators.

At provider level, more attention is needed on indicators of quality of care, and basic information around patient safety. For instance, there is no national system for adverse event reporting, and no information on hospital-acquired infections. Some quality indicators that are available at a national level, for instance the Health Care Quality Indicators (HCQI) data, should be able to be broken down to hospital level, but it is not clear whether these indicators are consistently used by policy makers, managers, or health care professionals.

Accessibility and quality of the Latvian health system

While there is much to commend in the Latvian health system, in the areas of access and quality there is more cause for concern. While the establishment of the NHS established universal health coverage for all Latvian residents, there are some clear problems around access. High levels of cost sharing for almost all service users create some financial barriers to access. Concentration of health services in urban areas creates geographical barriers to access, although Latvia is taking some steps to overcome them. Additionally, waiting times for services can be long. Many of these challenges are caused, or exacerbated, by Latvia's "quota" system for health care services.

Based on available indicators of quality, the Latvian primary care sector is performing relatively well, while there are more significant shortcomings in the hospital sector. For example, case fatality after stroke is almost three times higher than the OECD average. Low levels of investment in the health system make significant improvements to quality and access challenging, and some recommendations for reform will require additional resources. In terms of improving the accessibility and quality of the health system Latvia would benefit from OECD experiences.

There are both financial and geographical barriers to accessing health care, exacerbated by the annual "quota" system

Cost sharing for medical services are common across the Latvian health system, including for consultations and for prescriptions. Patients pay EUR 1.42 for each visit to a GP. In addition, a co-payment of up to EUR 42.77 was introduced in 2009 for inpatient surgical interventions, and patients also have to pay up to EUR 35.64 for various diagnostic and therapeutic services. In the same year, the cap on all co-payments for outpatient and inpatient health care services per person per year increased from about EUR 213 to EUR 570, and the cap on total payment per hospitalisation episode increased from EUR 114 to EUR 356. However, in 2010, co-payments for outpatient visits to specialists and hospitals were reduced from EUR 7.11 to EUR 4.27, and co-payments for daily inpatient charges in hospital were reduced from EUR 17 to EUR 13.52, starting from the second day (Taube et al., 2014).

Service providers are given annual quotas for the volume of services that will be paid for publicly, and when these limits are reached, patients must either wait for the following year and the renewal of the quota, or pay for the services out-of-pocket (or with private coverage). Paying out-of-pocket to avoid long waits for services, especially towards the end of the year, is common. As a result, the contribution of out-of-pocket funding in Latvia is substantially higher than in most OECD health systems, at 38.5% of total national expenditure on health in 2013. OOP medical spending represented 3.4% of final household consumption in Latvia in 2013, above the OECD average of 2.8%, and enough to be a significant barrier to many Latvians. The high co-payment for services is acknowledged by the Ministry of Health as stopping some 12-20% of Latvians from accessing health services. A recent survey found that 23.5% Latvians who forewent health care cited cost as the reason (Eurostat, 2015).

Previously, Latvia had taken steps to protect households from catastrophic health spending. Lower-income groups benefitted from increased financial protection under the Safety Net and Social Sector Reform Programme, introduced in October 2009. As part of the programme, certain households were temporarily exempt from health care co-payments, and subsidised pharmaceuticals were made available for the poorest households. However, at the end of the programme, in 2011, exemptions from user charges for low-income households ended.

EU fund investment for 2014-20, however, is particularly targeted to improving the health of people at risk of social exclusion and poverty. Latvia's Public Health Strategy for 2014-20, linked to the EU funds, focuses on four priority disease areas (cardiovascular disease, cancer, perinatal and neonatal health, and mental health) and include activities related to the design of the benefits package (including health technology assessment), organisation of service delivery, quality of care (including clinical pathways and guidelines), human resource and capital investment planning, and health promotion and disease prevention.

Particular attention is being paid to tackling mental ill-health of the working-age population in order to help people with mental health problems perform at work or bring them back into the labour market, in line with the OECD Council's Recommendation on Integrated Mental Health, Skills and Work Policy. The Public Health Strategy for 2014-20 includes measures to improve access and quality of mental health care at all levels of the health system, with particular focus on those at risk of social exclusion. Mental health promotion has also been prioritised, especially in schools and other community institutions. This is complemented by work by the Centre for Disease Prevention and Control to monitor and improve emotional well-being in school children.

Latvia introduced its Safety Net and Social Sector Reform Programme in response to the sharp economic contraction it experienced after the 2008 global financial crisis. The programme, developed with World Bank assistance, was a far-reaching initiative to maintain access to social protection, education and health services, whilst realising savings and efficiency gains. Within the health sector, efforts were focused on reducing dependency on hospital services, through the development of outpatient services (including the introduction of medical care at home, a second nurse at family doctor practices and development of day hospitals), emergency medical assistance, care for pregnant women and children, as well as preventive measures. Home services for chronic illnesses were targeted at keeping down hospital admissions, and free hotel-type accommodation for poorer groups facilitated day and ambulatory care. The programme also provided additional funding for primary care, through increasing GP contracts with nurses, and allowing a second nurse to be hired by GPs. An advisory telephone service connecting patients to a doctor at their GP surgery was also introduced from 2011. Additionally, some exemptions from co-payments were introduced for low-income groups, although these have since been repealed.

In 2012 the World Bank carried out an assessment of the implementation of the Safety Net and Social Reform Programme. It found that overall it had a favourable impact on efficiency of health care services. Some of the programme's measures have been integrated into Latvia's basic health budget and thereby continued, including development of outpatient services.

Latvia also has problems with geographical access to care in rural areas. Such challenges are to be expected, given the falling population, migration of the younger generation to urban areas in Latvia and out of Latvia, and reports of GPs leaving rural areas given the declining population, or reaching retirement without being replaced. Geographical distribution of secondary and tertiary services through the country also poses a problem, with many services concentrated in urban areas and particularly in or around Riga. The introduction of free hotel-type accommodation for low-income groups when they travel from home for treatment (typically for day surgery), introduced as part of the Safety Net and Social Sector Reform Programme, should mitigate this problem in part.

Beyond financial and geographical barriers, Latvia's annual quota system is an additional significant problem for access. The Ministry of Health requires that providers plan activity to be equally distributed across the year, and regularly publishes hospitals' waiting times. Nevertheless, in the final months of the year it can be very difficult to access all non-emergency services, with backlogs that cannot be cleared until the following year. The impact of this policy is seen on waiting times for services throughout the year, not just towards the end of the year.

More broadly, evidence of lengthy waiting times in Latvia is available. After admission for hip fracture, for example, only 50% of patients in Latvia have surgery within two days, compared to above 80% in most OECD countries. For cancer care, while the average time for referral from GP to specialist is relatively fast – ten days on average – time from diagnosis to start of treatment is much longer, typically 30 days across all cancers, compared to an average waiting time of 14-21 days in Hungary, or 7-21 days in the Slovak Republic (OECD, 2013a).

Some procedures are not publicly funded at all. Latvia's "positive list" for pharmaceuticals and procedures excludes certain services and goods from NHS coverage. The benefit basket is determined by both "positive lists" (for pharmaceuticals, and for certain diagnostic, preventive and therapeutic interventions under Regulations No. 1529) and negative lists (exclusion of certain services under Regulations No. 1529, including dental care for adults, rehabilitation with exceptions, sight and hearing correction aids). The coverage of products and services reimbursed by NHS is decided based on health technology assessment which evaluates affordability and cost efficiency for pharmaceutical goods, but systematic assessment for medical devices and procedures is not carried out. Coverage was reduced in the aftermath of the global financial crisis in 2008 in order to contain health spending during the austerity period.

The scope of NHS coverage is relatively limited. Procedures that might be expected to be covered, for example thoracic surgery and some neurological procedures, are not included. Overall, some clear gaps exist between national clinical guidelines and the publicly-funded benefits package. While the need to control spending is clear in the Latvian health system, without making such services and goods systematically available, access and the quality of care will suffer.

To some degree, waiting times could be accepted as a way of managing demand for care, and balancing demand with available resources. Already, Latvia does have some mechanisms in place that prioritise services for those with the greatest need, for example children and pregnant women (Mitenbergs et al., 2012). Nevertheless, the fact that the quotas for services are exhausted by the end of the year may suggest that quota levels are insufficient, and that investment is needed to raise the threshold. Carefully assessing the relationship between demand, waiting lists, and the rate at which quotas of services are consumed is a first step.

Regarding geographical barriers to health care, there are several steps that Latvia could take. First, the potential problems associated with geographical barriers in accessing care could be better understood if a broader range of data were systematically collected and reported. Second, based on more data on health professionals and estimated future demand, Latvia needs a mix of measures to develop and adequately distribute human resources, to tackle the foreseen shortage of certain health professionals, and to develop human resource skills. Such elements could be brought together in a comprehensive workforce plan. Finally, new and innovative ways of maximising the utility of existing health resources for rural populations could be considered. This should include maximising the contribution of all health professionals. Pharmacists, for instance, could take on a greater role in managing chronic conditions, and the role of nurses and *feldshers* (physician assistants) should be expanded.

Regarding financial barriers to health care, it is unlikely that cost sharing can be reduced substantially without an increase in other sources of revenue, principally public funds. Nonetheless, there are some steps that Latvia could take to improve the financial protection of households from health care costs. As a priority, it should conduct an assessment of the feasibility, and potential impact, of expanding cost-sharing exemptions. Re-introducing exemptions to low-income households and to patients with chronic conditions are two avenues for consideration.

Quality of care is mixed

"Avoidable admissions" for diabetes and COPD are both below the OECD average, suggesting that the primary care sector is providing effective management in the community for these conditions. The age-sex standardised rate for hospital admission for COPD is 161.7 per 100 000 population compared with the OECD average of 198.4 per 100 000 population. Latvia's rate of hospital admission for diabetes is also lower than that of the OECD average, at 131.2 compared with 149.8 per 100 000 population. In contrast, however, stands Latvia's high rate of hospital admission for asthma, which is 95.2 per 100 000 population, compared with the OECD average of 43.8 per 100 000 population (OECD, 2015a).

Indicators of the quality of care in hospitals give more cause for concern. For mortality following both AMI and stroke, Latvia has the highest or second-highest rate of death when ranked alongside OECD health systems. Furthermore, mortality following AMI and stroke (using the more robust patient-based, rather than hospital-based, indicators) worsened between 2008 and 2013, although this may to some extent reflect improved data accuracy. Mortality in the 30 days following AMI or stroke is a good indicator of quality of health care, capturing processes of care such as timely transport of patients and the delivery of effective treatment, for example thrombolytic treatment, and care in dedicated stroke or cardiac units. These indicators suggest there are important shortcomings in the quality of acute care in Latvia.

The low level of public spending on health contributes to poor quality and outcomes of care. As well as funding the health system more generously, however, there are important steps that Latvia should take to strengthen quality assurance and improvement. At present, quality assurance in Latvia is focused almost exclusively on patient safety and minimum standards, secured primarily through the Health Inspectorate, and the State Agency for Medicines. Some quality improvement initiatives are in place, for example participation of acute hospitals in voluntary accreditation, but these efforts are limited and sporadic.

Action around acute or secondary care quality is particularly needed. Attention should turn towards strengthening quality assurance mechanisms, and encouraging quality improvement. Many of the initial building blocks of a quality assurance architecture are in place – workforce training in compliance with EU regulations, regular inspections of all providers – including GPs – from an independent inspectorate, a requirement that providers establish "quality strategies" for each year, hospital accreditation systems, clinical guidelines, and efforts to reflect patients' views through patient satisfaction surveys and meetings with consumer and user groups. However, there is clear scope for further steps to build quality assurance and drive attention to quality improvement.

A closer review of clinical processes in Latvia – for example through further use and development of performance and outcome indicators – would help narrow the focus to particular areas for attention. The first step for Latvia would be to start reporting on all OECD Health Care Quality Indicators, to give a fuller overview of quality of care. At the same time, developing and reporting quality indicators at the provider level would help give Latvia a fuller understanding of differences in performance between providers. For instance, one of the things that would help Latvia understand why case fatality rates for AMI and stroke are so much higher than in OECD countries would be more granular data at the provider level.

Actions should be taken around the use and completeness of clinical guidelines. While clear and commendable progress has been made in developing and approving guidelines, the number of clinical guidelines in use remains relatively limited when compared to OECD countries, and there is not a systematic effort to understand nationally, regionally and locally, what percentage of care is delivered in line with clinical guidelines. If adherence to guidelines is found to be poor, either across the board or in particular areas, efforts to understand whether this is because of provider and practitioner resistance, lack of awareness of clinical guidelines, or because treatments recommended in guidelines are not covered in full by the reimbursement schedule. There are OECD countries at the forefront of clinical guideline development and innovation from whom Latvia could learn. In Denmark, for example, clinical guidelines describe not only “what should be done”, but they tend to describe “who should do what, when and where”.

Developing rigorous standards of care for providers is another priority for Latvia. At present, there are very few established standards for health care provision, and those that exist are mostly minimum-standard process checks, for example staffing numbers and facility checks. Latvia is struggling to find a robust framework for quality that could be used to apply minimum standards to all providers, regardless of their size and nature.

In Australia, the introduction of a comprehensive set of national safety and quality standards has had some success, and could be a good model for Latvia to follow. The standards were set up by the Australian Commission on Safety and Quality in Health Care (ACSQHC) to drive care of a uniformly high quality across the country. They are applied to all hospitals (private and public, across all states), covering ten priority areas including quality governance, hospital-acquired infection, medication safety and clinical handover (see Box 2.5 for further detail). There has been broad agreement from stakeholders that the new standards are a positive move forward, promoting greater clinical involvement and more directly addressing specific quality issues than other standards. The standards are acute-care focused, and it is acknowledged that further development is required to effectively apply the standards to non-hospital care, including primary care, aged care, mental health care and community care. Adherence to the standards is checked as part of hospitals’ accreditation process, carried out by a range of different accrediting bodies all of which are, in turn, are accredited by the ACSQHC (OECD, 2015g).

In addition to taking further steps to assure that minimum standards are being met, Latvia could do more to foster quality improvement. The availability and use of appropriate data will be vital to quality improvement efforts, and benchmarking providers on performance metrics can encourage competition on quality. Performance metrics when contracting with hospitals could also be introduced, as is the case in Denmark, Portugal and Sweden. These performance criteria could be linked to specific payment mechanisms or budgets, and would serve to make quality of care an integrated part of the local and national governance arrangements, and a way of using performance data more actively.

Encouraging excellence through the application of a broader array of quality incentives should also be considered. Latvia has already begun to do this in primary care with the introduction of a pay-for-performance scheme. The compulsory scheme, introduced in 2013, consists of 13 criteria. GPs must meet individual annual targets in the domains of prevention, treatment of patients with a chronic condition, increased cost efficiency of health care services, and the diversity of procedures and other services GPs provide.

The average quality-linked payment issued to family doctors in 2013 was EUR 355, accounting for a very small portion of GPs' total annual income. This may suggest that the current system is providing insufficient motivation for GPs to improve quality: data show that at least half of GPs fulfilled the quality criteria in only five of the 13 indicators. Latvia may need to increase the incentives given to GPs to drive quality improvements. In addition, the indicators mainly relate to the process of care, rather than patient outcomes. In this, once GPs have grown accustomed to the existing performance framework, there may be scope to expand it to take in more indicators related to clinical practice and patient outcomes.

To improve the quality of hospital care, Latvia could look to strategies adopted by some OECD countries, including introducing performance metrics when contracting with hospitals, broadening the use and effectiveness of performance-based payment and other financial incentives, strengthening the voluntary accreditation system in hospitals and expanding it to other providers, and reflecting on clinical processes through clinical audits. Latvia intends to introduce a national health care quality assurance system as one of the investment priorities linked to EU funds for 2014-20.

Portugal, for example, has introduced new models of hospital management with the transformation of public hospitals into public enterprises giving more managerial and financial autonomy. This was accompanied by a new payment system that created explicit separation between the purchaser and the provider of hospital services. Prospective global budgets based on negotiated contracts are allocated to NHS public hospitals. The global budget is made up of an activity-based prospective payment involving systematic DRG grouping and case-mix adjustment for inpatient and ambulatory surgery (the DRG component accounts for nearly 50% of hospital financing), while the remaining hospital revenue comes from fee-for-services (for outpatient and emergency visits), bundled payments (for some chronic conditions), and some quality-based payments. Since 2011, each hospital has to establish a three-year action plan for hospital reorganisation with the Regional Health Authority so that reform implementation can be continuously monitored by regional authorities. Overall, the results of the past and ongoing hospital reforms have had positive impacts on both quality and efficiency (OECD, 2015c).

Latvia's initiatives to strengthen primary care and promote continuity of care have been particularly innovative

Latvia has undertaken several initiatives to strengthen the quality of primary care. To overcome geographical barriers to care, for example, GPs receive a bonus for maintaining a practice in rural areas. The bonus is based on the density of the population in a given area, and the number of registered patients. Complementing this policy, in more densely populated areas a second nurse or physician assistant is now mandatory for practices with more than 1 800 registered patients or 800 registered children. The additional staff are tasked to focus on prevention and discuss life-style risk factors such as, for example, smoking and harmful alcohol consumption.

Initiatives have also been introduced to strengthen primary care quality. A compulsory pay-for-performance scheme was introduced in 2013, in which GPs must meet individual annual targets around prevention, treatment of chronic conditions, increased efficiency, and the diversity of services that they provide. Targets, however, mainly relate to the process of care, rather than patient outcomes. To promote early diagnosis, GPs can receive payments of EUR 71.14 per patient to detect first and second-stage cancer in registered patients. Latvia also introduced an alert system to inform GPs by email about patients who called for emergency medical assistance but were not hospitalised. The GP is obliged to contact such patients and agree upon the course of treatment to ensure continuity of care.

Each of these initiatives is underpinned by an ambitious national Primary Care Development Plan for 2014-16. This addresses twelve priority activities, including reforms to financing and better information systems, with the overall aim of strengthening accessibility and co-ordination, improving quality and safety, and improving information and support to patients.

Although wide ranging and ambitious, the impact of such initiatives is not always evident. As noted earlier, key risk factors are worsening in Latvia and cancer screening rates remain low, signalling a failure of prevention. Of some concern, in the pay-for-performance scheme mentioned above, most indicators were failed by most GPs. The scheme is relatively new and hopefully GPs' performance will improve quickly. Underlying reasons for poor performance need to be identified, however. One pertinent fact is likely to be the near-negligible payments attached to the scheme. Many of Latvia's quality and performance initiatives risk being held back without more generous resourcing of the health system, as discussed in the next section.

Efficiency and sustainability in the Latvian health system

Since the global financial crisis in 2008, severe budget consolidation measures and efficiency-enhancing measures were taken in Latvia's health system. In the hospital sector, developments such as payment reforms, concentration of specialised care, and reorganisation of emergency care through a centralised triage system, were made. However, there are still a number of challenges to address, including maintaining the supply of health care workers. Without bringing public spending on health closer to OECD averages, it is likely that the performance and sustainability of Latvia's health system will be seriously jeopardised.

Latvia has taken impressive steps towards improving efficiency in the hospital sector

In a system that is structurally under-funded, increasing efficiency to maximise the impact of limited resources has been, and continues to be, a major priority in Latvia. There has been some impressive progress. Most strikingly, Latvia has closed a number of hospitals and 18 emergency departments to improve quality and contain costs. Simultaneous efforts were made to move care out of hospitals to community settings, to reduce admissions and length of stay in hospitals, and to prioritise outpatient care.

Bed numbers and average length of hospital stay have both declined substantially, as earlier described. This was due to the closure of some institutions, and the transformation of others to providing outpatient services. Financing from EU funds in 2007-13 was channelled towards improving the skills and knowledge of practitioners, transforming small hospitals into outpatient facilities and developing the infrastructure of the bigger hospitals. Between 2005 and 2013, there was also a decrease of nearly 15% in average duration of treatment at inpatient institutions,. The number of outpatient visits, including visits to primary and secondary care specialists, increased by 19% between 2005 and 2010.

Hospital payment mechanisms have been changed since 2010, with efforts to reward efficiency introduced, and the introduction of DRGs in 2015. To ensure timely access to acute care, emergency care has been reorganised and now the country has a centralised and standardised triage system. In addition, some local examples of innovation in driving efficiency are commendable. One example is the introduction of an "observation ward" in all emergency hospitals (as in Vidzemes Hospital in the Valmiera district, described in Chapter 2). Such innovation is an encouraging sign for Latvia, and suggests that governance arrangements leave room for dynamic thinking, and responsiveness to local needs. Also, commendably, local hospitals seem to collaborate well with other local providers, including hospitals nearby, in seeking efficient ways of providing care at a regional level.

More strategic and stable planning to promote efficiency and sustainability is needed, particularly around the hospital sector and the health workforce

The challenges that Latvia will face in the next 10-20 years – an ageing population, a rise in chronic disease, a likely rise in obesity – demand reflection, planning and action now. Longer-term strategic policy planning is also needed to inform capital investment beyond the current one-year budgets. When reflecting on future priorities, and changing health care needs, Latvia's relatively under-funded approach to prevention should raise particular concerns. Fortunately, the Public Health Strategy for 2014-20 (focussing on perinatal and neonatal health, mental health, cardiovascular, and oncological diseases as earlier mentioned), allocates considerable financial resources for health promotion and prevention activities, from both EU funds and state budget.

Firstly, a strategic approach to further efficiency gains in the hospital sector is needed. While Latvia has already reduced acute hospital beds and closed a number of hospitals and emergency departments, more changes will be needed in order to secure high-quality care that represents good value for money. Difficult decisions and compromises will need to be made, continuing to balance the priority of assuring appropriate access to services for all Latvians, and the need to close hospitals with lower activity rates to promote quality and efficiency gains. A starting point would be a comprehensive mapping of services (hospital, outpatient, community and primary), including service volumes, to assess where there is slack in the system. Such an exercise would help pinpoint where services can be closed, or adapted. Latvia undertook a similar exercise prior to the reform of the emergency care system, assessing which departments were not representing good value for money, or delivering high quality.

Reflection on the ownership of Latvian hospitals is needed. While it is apparent that some municipal governments, and local populations, may be very invested in their local hospital, there is an argument to be made for transferring ownership (or functional governance) of all hospitals to the central level. Such a move would allow for a more integrated, national system for ownership and management of hospital estates. It would also allow a more strategic planning to be undertaken, and could also give hospitals more freedom to develop more enterprising approaches to quality and efficiency improvements.

More strategic contracting, to promote efficiency and quality, should also be pursued by the NHS. The NHS could strengthen monitoring and evaluation of provider activities, selectively contracting with better-performing providers to drive quality improvement. In the same vein, the NHS could look to contract more often with independent providers, on clear cost/quality criteria, with expected outcomes specified in contracts. Selective purchasing could be applied also by the private voluntary health insurance schemes by focusing not only the cost but also the quality aspects of health care. Alongside these efforts, public reporting of provider assessment should also be developed as such information could be used to promote user choice of provider.

A mid- to longer-term strategic NHS plan should also address workforce challenges. Such a plan should consider training needs, based on expected retirement rates. Geographical shortages of health professionals should be considered, and Latvia could consider targeting recruitment for training towards populations in rural and under-served areas who may be more likely to wish to return to practice in the area. Remuneration and working conditions – particularly for nurses – need consideration. Latvia's nurses have some of the lowest salaries in the OECD – an estimated USD 6 000 per year, compared to the OECD average of USD PPP 45 000. Appropriate ways of expanding professional roles to meet changing needs, and maximising workforce contribution, should also be included. For example, pharmacists could contribute more to care for patients with chronic conditions in the community, and the role of nurses could be expanded into areas such as prevention and health promotion. Initiatives to increase the contribution of the nursing workforce are being considered, but reports suggest that logistical challenges – such as the unavailability of a room for nurses to work in – is limiting the impact of this change.

Latvia could become a more data-driven system, with health system information used to drive planning, quality and efficiency

Latvia could do more to become a more data-driven health system, in terms of both available data, and the way the data are used. In particular, more attention is still needed on indicators of quality of care. There is no national system for adverse event reporting, for example, and no information on hospital-acquired infections. Some quality indicators are available at a national level, and should be able to be broken down to a hospital level, but it is not clear that these indicators are consistently used by policy makers, managers, or health care professionals. Information on care quality at primary care level is also weak.

More broadly, Latvia has not exploited the possibilities of using health information to the fullest for evidence-based policy making and quality improvement. For example, Latvia conducts only a few health-related surveys, while many OECD countries use surveys as important tools to collect a wide range of information including on patient experience, care co-ordination and patient safety. Developing more complete, more granular and better linked provider-data systems will be a key step for Latvia in more fully addressing efficiency, waste, and care quality. In a resource-stretched country like Latvia, not only can such advances in data exploitation bring greater value for money from spending, but it is also very likely a less costly way of promoting quality than some other possible quality levers, for instance resource-intensive accreditation or clinical audit programmes.

At a local level, the NHS could undertake more systematic monitoring and assessment of health provider performance and health care utilisation by using information collected through e-health. This could be done as part of promoting better quality of care and adequate use of health care resources as done in some OECD countries such as Denmark and Portugal. Better data can also be used as part of reducing waste in the system, and improving the effective use of resources. For example, provider-level data can be used to identify variations in care and outcomes. While medical treatment should be based on clinical evidence, need and patient preferences, there is strong evidence that care provision is not solely explained by these factors; geographical variations in care can be significant, even when robust national clinical guidelines exist. A better understanding of variations can be used to help prevent costly over-provision of care, and harmful under-provision.

Sustainability and health system strengthening will be ongoing challenges without further investment

Significant progress across any of the areas outlined above will be extremely difficult given the current level of resources in the system. While some improvements may bring efficiency gains, most will involve at least a certain level of upfront investment. To push towards performance and care quality on a par with most OECD countries, more investment will be needed. Low and unstable levels of financing will undermine continued consistent improvements, and reliance on EU funding for some core areas – notably prevention and health promotion – is a challenge to sustainable growth, and impedes the development of a clear long-term vision for the health system.

To start seeing health outcomes closer to the OECD average, and make real inroads into problems with access and quality, Latvia will most likely need to increase health spending per capita to a level closer to the OECD average, and almost certainly to increase the share of GDP spent on health closer to the OECD average. A targeted, incremental increase in spending is needed, rather than a sudden cash injection, which would bring significant risks and likely limited return over time. Support from the OECD, other international partners, and OECD countries could be offered to help Latvia manage the increase in health spending to maximise the positive impact (Box 0.2).

Box 0.2. Recommendations for health system performance strengthening in Latvia: Access, quality, efficiency, sustainability

To improve the performance of the health system, across the domains of access, quality, efficiency, and sustainability, Latvia should:

1. Improve access to health care, by:

a) Taking steps to reduce economic and geographical barriers to health care:

- Co-payments are a significant barrier to access. As a priority, steps should be taken to ensure that ability to pay is not a factor in accessing health care. Exemptions to low-income households and to patients with chronic conditions should be re-introduced, after assessing the feasibility and impact of expanding cost-sharing exemptions;
- Better data on workforce supply, service utilisation and unmet needs are needed to understand problems associated with barriers to access, and better distribute health system resources to match needs. In particular, reasons underlying low uptake of breast and cervical cancer screening should be investigated.

b) Reflecting on whether the "quota" system for organising and reimbursing health care is fit-for-purpose:

- Reassessing the reimbursement list for services, to ensure that the publicly-covered benefits basket is consistent with latest international best practice;
- Exploring the impact of the quotas on waiting times throughout the year, and assessing whether higher quotas are required for some services, such as cancer care, and diagnostic and therapeutic procedures for heart disease, given Latvia's high fatality rates.

c) Expanding training capacity to train medical graduates in primary care and better developing the roles of other primary care professionals such as nurses and pharmacists.

2. Focus on quality of health care provision, by:

a) Strengthening the basic quality architecture to go beyond assessing compliance with minimum standards and move towards continuous quality improvement. Areas to focus on include:

- Critically evaluating the Annual Quality Assessment scheme in primary care to understand reasons for its initially modest impact on primary care performance, and developing further cycles of the scheme appropriately ;
- Implementing quality indicators, linked to standards and guidelines, in other health care sectors, including mental health care and community services; and
- Building a system of national disease or patient registers as the backbone of any quality improvement initiative.

b) Working with professional and patient groups to develop robust, open reporting of quality and outcomes across clinics and hospitals. Understanding provider-level variation will be critical to addressing Latvia's poor survival rates after heart attack or stroke, for example.

c) Developing a national adverse event reporting and learning system, to include health care-associated infections. England's experience in building and using such a system would be an informative model to study.

Box 0.2. Recommendations for health system performance strengthening in Latvia: Access, quality, efficiency, sustainability *(cont.)*

d) Broadening the indicators that Latvia systematically collects on quality of care; in particular, prioritising the reporting of international benchmarks such as the OECD's Health Care Quality Indicators. A particular focus on the effectiveness of secondary prevention is needed, by comparing rates of avoidable hospitalisation and the quality of prescribing in primary care.

e) Putting the right quality improvement incentives in place, through:

- Introducing performance metrics when contracting with hospitals;
- Broadening the use and effectiveness of performance-based payment and other financial incentives;
- Strengthening the voluntary accreditation system for hospitals, to identify excellence rather than just adherence to minimum requirements, and expanding it to other providers;
- Increasing patients' and the public's involvement in provider inspection and accreditation;
- Reflecting on clinical processes through clinical audits, drawing on the Nordic countries' experience of using national disease or patient registers, for example, to monitor and improve quality and outcomes.

3. Drive efficiency gains, by:

a) Ensuring that the NHS is more than a passive distributor of funds, and instead develops its capacity for strategic contracting, actively monitoring and incentivising quality and efficiency in its contracts with providers.

b) Looking for ways to reduce waste and inefficiency in the health system, including:

- Better understanding health care needs, activities, outcomes and costs across pathways of care, by linking data at individual level across databases held by health and social care providers;
- Working with clinicians and service managers to develop robust, open reporting of productivity and efficiency indicators across clinics and hospitals, such as patient readmission rates, or staff sickness-absence rates;
- Ensuring effective use of pharmaceuticals – particularly promoting use of generics – and medical devices – appropriate distribution country-wide – as well as reflection on procurement processes and payment systems;
- Considering the lessons of the *Choosing Wisely* initiative, which distils complex clinical guidelines into guidance for doctors and patients on when to use tests and treatments, in an effort to improve quality and reduce waste.

c) Balancing the benefits of hospitals' autonomy and state-owned enterprise status with the strategic steer of a national plan for the development and use of the hospital sector. This plan should consider:

- The size and structure of the hospital estate, demonstrating leadership in further rationalising specialist services beyond the gains already achieved in reducing hospital bed numbers;

Box 0.2. Recommendations for health system performance strengthening in Latvia: Access, quality, efficiency, sustainability *(cont.)*

- Ownership and accountabilities around hospital services. In particular, consideration should be given to whether municipalities are the right level of government to hold accountability for hospital performance. Transferring this to central government would support national planning and, by pooling capacity and expertise, may spur innovation in service delivery.
- Planning and co-ordination for primary and community care, which would be impacted by reconfigurations of specialist services.

d) Considering how best to make use of the additional capacity offered by private sector providers. Contracting with more private sector providers should be based on clear cost and quality selection criteria, with outcomes pre-specified in contracts. National standards and guidelines for care, as described earlier, will be needed to underpin this.

4. Ensure health system sustainability, by:

a) Undertaking a spending review, with a view to increasing public spending on health. To see health outcomes closer to the OECD average, and make real inroads into problems with access and quality, Latvia will most likely need to increase health spending to a level closer to the OECD average.

b) Developing a comprehensive five or ten-year plan setting out the expected strategic direction for the health service, which may help promote sustainable and consistent policy making against an often unstable political backdrop.

c) Establishing a comprehensive workforce plan to facilitate sustainable development of human resources in the health sector, which would need to be backed by appropriate levels of resources to be effective.

d) Ensuring that long-term care is adequately developed, to effectively respond to changing care needs as the population ages.

References

CDPC – Centre for Disease Prevention and Control (2014), *Statistical Yearbook of Health Care in Latvia 2013*, Riga.

Eurostat Database (2015), http://ec.europa.eu/eurostat/data/database.

Hazans, M. (2011), "Labour Market Integration in Latvia", in M. Kahanec and K.F. Zimmermann (eds.), *Ethnic Diversity in European Labour Markets*, Edward Elgar Publishing.

IARC – International Agency for Research on Cancer (2015), *Country Factsheets: Latvia*, http://eu-cancer.iarc.fr/eucan/Country.aspx?ISOCountryCd=428.

Mitenbergs, U. et al (2012), "Latvia: Health System Review", *Health Systems in Transition*, Vol. 14, No. 8, pp. 1–191.

OECD (2015a), *Health at a Glance 2015: OECD Indicators*, OECD Publishing, Paris, http://dx.doi.org/ 10.1787/19991312.

OECD (2015b), *OECD Reviews of Health Care Quality: Japan 2015: Raising Standards*, OECD Publishing, Paris, http://dx.doi.org/10.1787/9789264225817-en.

OECD (2015c), *OECD Reviews of Health Care Quality: Portugal 2015: Raising Standards*, OECD Publishing, Paris, http://dx.doi.org/10.1787/9789264225985-en.

OECD (2015d), "Focus on Health Spending: OECD Health Statistics 2015", OECD, Paris, http://www.oecd.org/health/health-systems/Focus-Health-Spending-2015.pdf.

OECD (2015e), *OECD Health Statistics 2015*, OECD Publishing, Paris, http://dx.doi.org/10.1787/health-data-en.

OECD (2015f), *International Migration Outlook 2015*, OECD Publishing, Paris, http://dx.doi.org/10.1787/migr_outlook-2015-en.

OECD (2015g), *OECD Reviews of Health Care Quality: Australia 2015: Raising Standards*, OECD Publishing, Paris, http://dx.doi.org/10.1787/9789264233836-en.

OECD (2013a), *Cancer Care: Assuring Quality to Improve Survival*, OECD Health Policy Studies, OECD Publishing, Paris, http://dx.doi.org/10.1787/9789264181052-en.

OECD (2013b), *International Migration Outlook 2013*, OECD Publishing, Paris, http://dx.doi.org/10.1787/migr_outlook-2013-en.

Taube, M., U. Mitenbergs and A. Sagan (2014), *The Impact of the Financial Crisis on the Health System and Health in Latvia*, World Health Organization (acting as the host organisation for, and secretariat of, the European Observatory on Health Systems and Policies).

Chapter 1

Health and health care in Latvia

As a result of the global financial crisis in 2008, Latvia was forced to implement substantial measures to limit public spending. The hospital and emergency care sectors were reorganised, leading to efficiency gains. Primary care was also strengthened, with the aim of focusing more effort on preventive care. OECD countries can learn from successful Latvian initiatives in these areas.

Latvia still has markedly poorer health, however, compared to other OECD countries. Population ageing and worsening rates of smoking and other key risk factors mean that more people are living with chronic disease, and demands on the health system are intensifying. Latvia must continue to undertake reforms, therefore, to optimise performance of the health care system and improve people's health.

This chapter describes the Latvian health system with respect to governance, revenue collection and purchasing, service delivery models, and the information infrastructure underlying these functions. Key challenges in each of these areas are identified.

The statistical data for Israel are supplied by and under the responsibility of the relevant Israeli authorities. The use of such data by the OECD is without prejudice to the status of the Golan Heights, East Jerusalem and Israeli settlements in the West Bank under the terms of international law.

Introduction

Latvia's health care system is tasked with tackling a significantly larger burden of ill-health compared to most other OECD countries, with significantly fewer resources. Life expectancy is low, due to high rates of premature death and disability from non-communicable diseases, road traffic accidents, mental illness and suicide. Key risk factors such as smoking and harmful alcohol consumption are worsening, rather than being controlled. Yet, only around 5% of GDP is spent on health care, with nearly 40% of this coming from out-of-pocket sources.

Universal health coverage has been achieved, however, through a single-purchaser national health system, which access to a relatively full range of basic and specialist health care services. A purchaser-provider split is in place, and Latvia has successfully reduced its dependence on the hospital sector. Nevertheless, strains are apparent. The shortage of hospital specialists in rural areas is a particularly pressing example.

This chapter describes first the population health and health care needs in Latvia. Section 1.2 describes the main features of Latvia's health system, and the roles and challenges of its principal stakeholders. The final section discusses how health system revenues are raised and allocated, and challenges related to the efficient use of resources.

1.1. Population health and health care needs in Latvia

Population health in Latvia is still relatively poor compared to other OECD countries. Life expectancy is low, and although population ageing is progressing more slowly than in many OECD countries, health and long-term care needs amongst the elderly remain high. Together, these drivers place substantial pressure on the Latvian health system.

Large numbers of working-age Latvians have left the country in recent years

The population of Latvia peaked at almost 2.7 million around 1990. Since then, it has dropped by almost 30%, falling to less than 2.1 million in 2013 (Figure 1.1). This phenomenon has largely been driven by emigration of the working-age population to other European countries, following independence in 1991 and the global financial crisis in 2008. Since 2000, Latvia lost 14% of its working-age population; between 2008 and 2013, 30 000 people left every year, especially the young and well-educated (Hazans, 2011; OECD, 2013b; OECD, 2015c). Population decline is expected to continue over the next few decades because of low fertility rates and continuing emigration. In 2013, the fertility rate was 1.5 children per women aged 15-49, slightly lower than the OECD average of 1.7 (OECD, 2015e).

Latvia's health professionals have also migrated to other European countries. The expatriation rate for Latvian doctors (3.1% in 2010/11) was lower, however, than the OECD average (4.1%) and European Union average (6.3%). In contrast, the expatriation rate for Latvian nurses was more comparable (at 5.0% vs. OECD average 2.8% and EU average of 4.9%; OECD, 2015c). Nevertheless, the density of doctors and nurses per 1 000 population has remained broadly stable in Latvia, as discussed further in Section 1.3.

Figure 1.1. Population of Latvia, 1980-2050

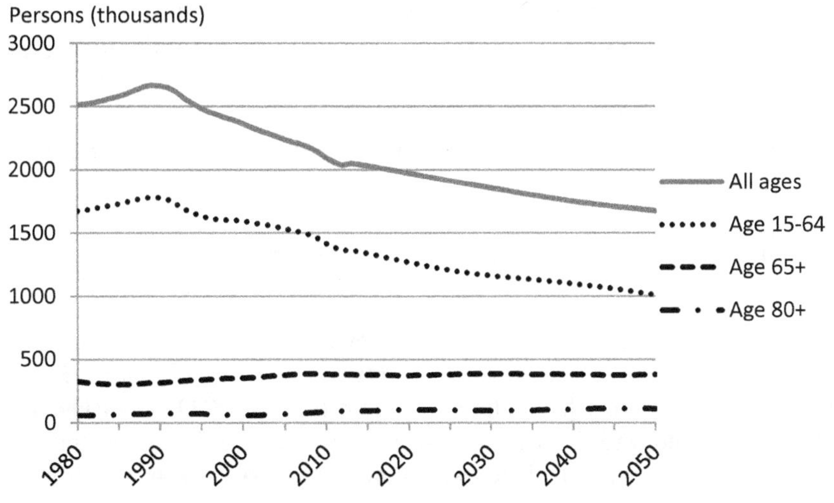

Population ageing is perhaps less of a challenge for Latvia than other OECD countries. Although the share of the population aged 65 and over is above the OECD average (18.6% vs 15.6% in 2013), population ageing is not expected to progress as fast as many OECD countries, despite Latvia's low fertility rate. This is partly due to the country's shorter life expectancy. In 2050, the share of the population aged 65 and over is expected to reach 22.8%, compared to the OECD average of 27.1%. The dependency ratio (of the population aged 65 and over to the population aged between 20 and 64) is also growing more slowly than the OECD average, and is projected to reach 41% in 2050 (Figure 1.2).

Figure 1.2. Dependency ratios in Latvia, 1980-2050

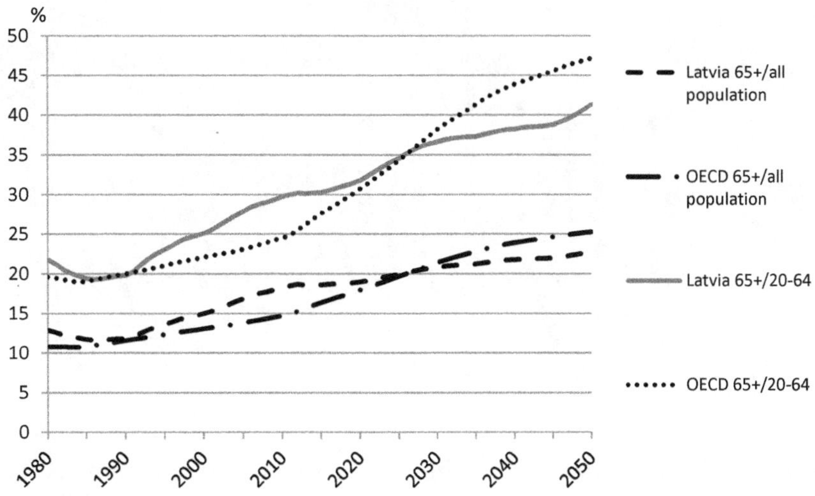

Source: Based on data from OECD (2015), *Pensions at a Glance: OECD and G20 Indicators*, Chapter 7, OECD Publishing, Paris, http://dx.doi.org/10.1787/pension_glance-2015-en.

Nevertheless, health care and long-term care needs of Latvia's elderly population are high and need to be addressed. Self-reported health status among the elderly is poorer than many OECD countries. Only 8.2% of people aged 65 and over reported that they were in good or very good health in 2013, around a fifth of the European average (38.7%; Eurostat, 2015). Larger proportions of the elderly in Latvia also reported limitations in daily activity and having a long-standing illness or health problem. As discussed in Chapter 2, however, access to health care remains problematic and the availability of long-term care does not appear sufficient.

General health status remains relatively poor, but maternal and child health is improving rapidly

Life expectancy at birth in Latvia remains lower than any other OECD country, at 73.9 years in 2013, compared with 80.5 years OECD average (Figure 1.3). Healthy life year expectancy at birth is also low relative to most other OECD countries, although it is higher than Estonia and the Slovak Republic for men, and higher than the Slovak Republic and Portugal for women. Life expectancy at age 65 is also much lower than the OECD average, at 18.6 years for women and 13.7 years for men, compared to 21.1 and 17.8 years OECD average, respectively.

Figure 1.3. Life expectancy at birth, 2013 (or nearest year)

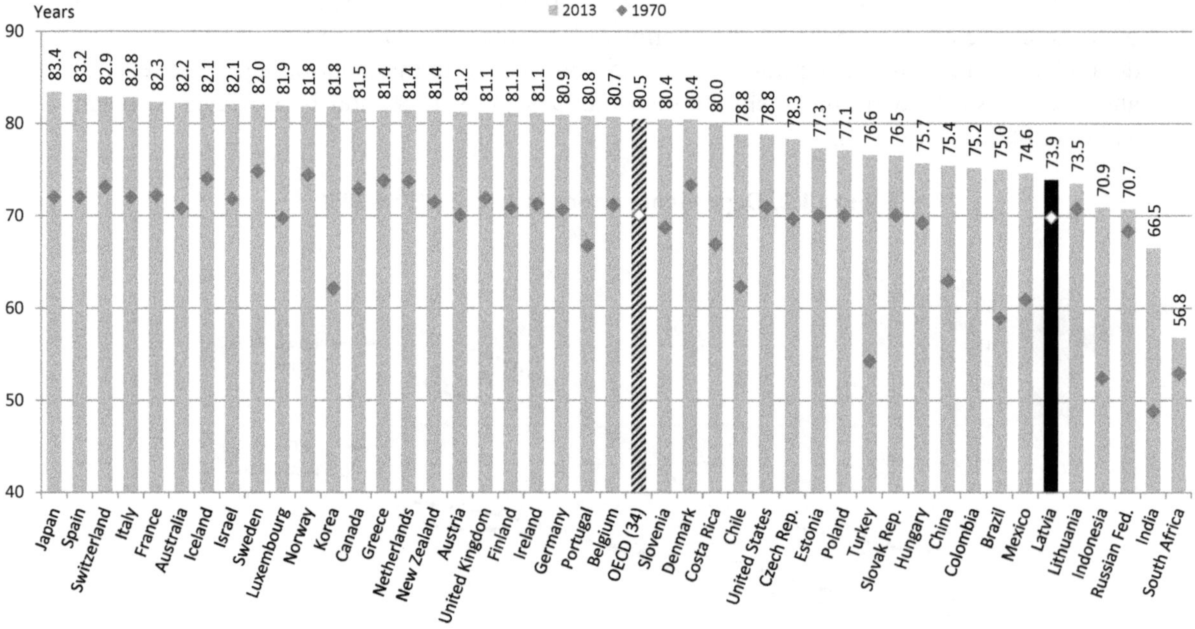

Source: OECD Health Statistics 2015, http://dx.doi.org/10.1787/health-data-en.

The gender gap in life expectancy at birth is 11 years – more than twice as large as the OECD average. The gender gap in life expectancy at age 65, at around five years, is also wider than any other OECD country. These large gaps are due to consistently higher mortality rates among men across all disease groups. Overall, the mortality rate for men is 1.9 times greater than the rate for women. Specifically, mortality for men is 6.9 times higher than women for suicide, 3.2 times higher for transport accidents, 2.1 times higher for cancer, 1.8 times higher for ischemic heart disease and 1.3 times higher for stroke

(OECD, 2015e). Disease incidence is also greater among men. For example, cancer incidence is about 60% higher for men in Latvia, but less than 10% in the United Kingdom, Denmark and Iceland (OECD, 2015b). These gender differences can partly be explained by the greater prevalence of risk factors among men in Latvia.

The shorter life expectancy in Latvia compared with other OECD countries is explained by high mortality rates from all major causes of death. Mortality rates from ischemic heart disease and stroke are both three times higher than the OECD average (at 357 per 100 000 population compared with 117 OECD average, and 200 per 100 000 population compared with 66 OECD average, in 2013). Mortality is also higher for cancer (245 per 100 000 population compared with 206 OECD average). Leading causes of cancer death are prostate cancer, lung cancer, bowel cancer, stomach cancer and bladder cancer for men; and breast cancer, bowel cancer, uterine cancer, cervical cancer and ovarian cancer for women (IARC, 2015). The suicide rate and mortality due to transport accidents are also both higher in Latvia than elsewhere in the OECD, at 20 per 100 000 population compared with 12 OECD average, and 10 per 100 000 population compared with 7 OECD average.

In terms of mortality from cardiovascular disease (CVD), Latvia followed the same downward trend as other OECD countries in the 2000s. The decline was rather rapid in Latvia in the 2000s (Figure 1.4), but CVD still accounts for a large share of all deaths. This is partly due to the high prevalence of risk factors, weaker prevention in primary care (Chapter 3) and limited coverage of cardiology procedures in health services reimbursed by public funding (Chapter 2). In recent years, mortality due to CVD has increased both in Latvia and across many OECD countries. This may be due to the increasing trend of obesity, diabetes and other related risk factors, underlining the importance of prevention and health promotion.

Figure 1.4. Mortality rates, between 2000 and 2013 (or nearest year)

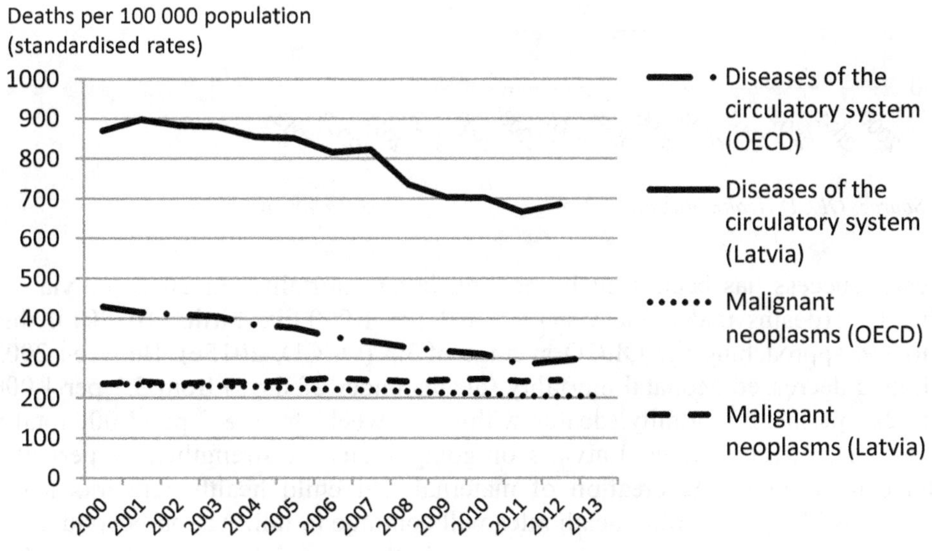

Source: OECD Health Statistics 2015, http://dx.doi.org/10.1787/health-data-en.

Mortality from cancer increased in Latvia since 2000, in contrast to the gradual decline in cancer mortality rates across the OECD on average during the same period. In particular, mortality rates from colorectal cancer, prostate cancer and cervical cancer have been increasing over the past decade in Latvia. This is partly due to low quality of cancer care – as reflected by low survival of breast, cervical and colorectal cancer, compared to many OECD countries. In terms of breast cancer, the incidence rate is low, but the mortality rate is slightly higher than the OECD average and this may be partly due to low screening coverage among women in target age group (Chapter 3), low and limited access to cancer drugs (OECD, 2013a).

Regarding external causes of death, Latvia has not always followed the general trend observed across OECD countries over the past decade. While most OECD countries steadily reduced mortality from transport accidents in the 2000s, Latvia's trajectory was mixed. Some years saw a larger decline than the OECD average, but in other years a slight increase was reported. In terms of suicide, mortality rates have also decreased steadily across OECD countries since 2000. The same trend was apparent in Latvia until 2007/08, when suicide rates increased (Figure 1.5).

Figure 1.5. Suicide rates, between 2000 and 2013 (or nearest year)

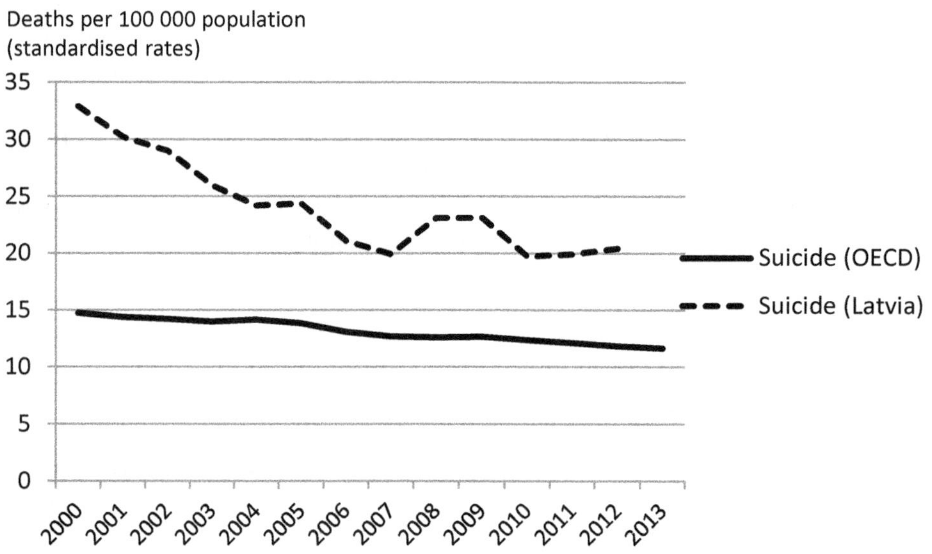

Source: OECD Health Statistics 2015, http://dx.doi.org/10.1787/health-data-en.

Greater success has been seen in tackling infant mortality. In 2012, Latvia's infant mortality rate (deaths under one year) was 6.3 per 1 000 live births. By 2014, this had fallen to 3.9, approaching the OECD average of 3.8 (OECD, 2015e). Between 2003 and 2013, Latvia decreased neonatal mortality (deaths under 28 days) from 5.7 per 1 000 live births to 2.5; perinatal mortality (deaths within one week) from 8.7 per 1 000 total births to 5.7 (OECD, 2015e). Given Latvia's on-going focus on strengthening perinatal and neonatal care, through the creation of maternal and child health networks and other initiatives, it is likely that infant death rates will continue to fall. Action beyond the health sector, that focusses on tackling low income and other social determinants of health, will also be needed (Schell et al., 2007). These factors represent persistent challenges to maternal and child health in Latvia (see below).

The burden of disease from some communicable diseases remains high, although vaccination coverage is good

Latvia also needs to tackle the spread of infectious disease. The incidence of HIV is one of the highest in Europe at 16.6 per 100 000 population in 2012. Consequently, the incidence of AIDS also high (at 6.8 per 100 000 population) and, of significant concern, increasing. In contrast, most OECD countries have managed to reduce the incidence of AIDS since the mid-1990s (Figure 1.6). In this context, Latvia recently approved additional funding for HIV/AIDS treatment. Incidence rates of hepatitis B is also high, with more than ten cases per 100 000 population, compared to the OECD average of two. More promisingly, vaccination rates against hepatitis B among children aged 1 has attained the OECD average, leading to a considerable reduction of incidence among children. This suggests that hepatitis B may be controlled in the future if the high vaccination coverage is maintained.

Figure 1.6. Trends in AIDS incidence rates, selected EU member states, 2002-13

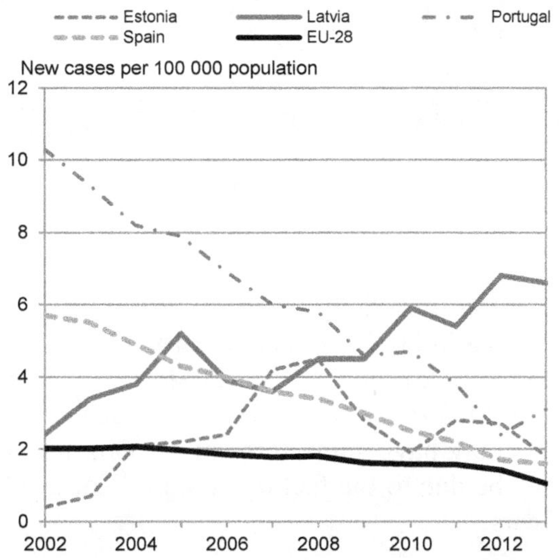

Source: ECDC and WHO Regional Office for Europe (2013), HIV/AIDS Surveillance in Europe 2012.

Vaccination rates for other communicable diseases such as diphtheria, tetanus, pertussis and measles have broadly matched OECD averages over the past decade. In 2013, the vaccination rate for diphtheria, tetanus and pertussis was the same level as the OECD average at 95% and the rate for measles was 96%, higher than the OECD average of 94% (OECD, 2015b).

The prevalence of key risk factors for non-communicable disease is worsening in Latvia

The smoking rate in Latvia is 34.3%, almost double the OECD average of 19.7% in 2013 (OECD, 2015e). Of particular concern, smoking rates have not fallen in Latvia over the past decade, as in most other OECD countries – in fact, they increased by just over 1%. Smoking is particularly concentrated in men, with more half smoking daily compared to less than one in five women. Nevertheless, smoking reduction has been achieved in the younger population. Between 2011 and 2014, use of tobacco products in children aged 13 to 15 decreased from 39.4% to 25.3% among boys and from 41.4% to 23.9% among girls. Prevalence of regular smoking of cigarettes in this age group also decreased from 29.5% to 16.9% among boys, and from 33.8% to 16.5% among girls (WHO Global Youth Tobacco Survey, forthcoming).

Figure 1.7. Daily smoking in adults, 2013 (or nearest year)

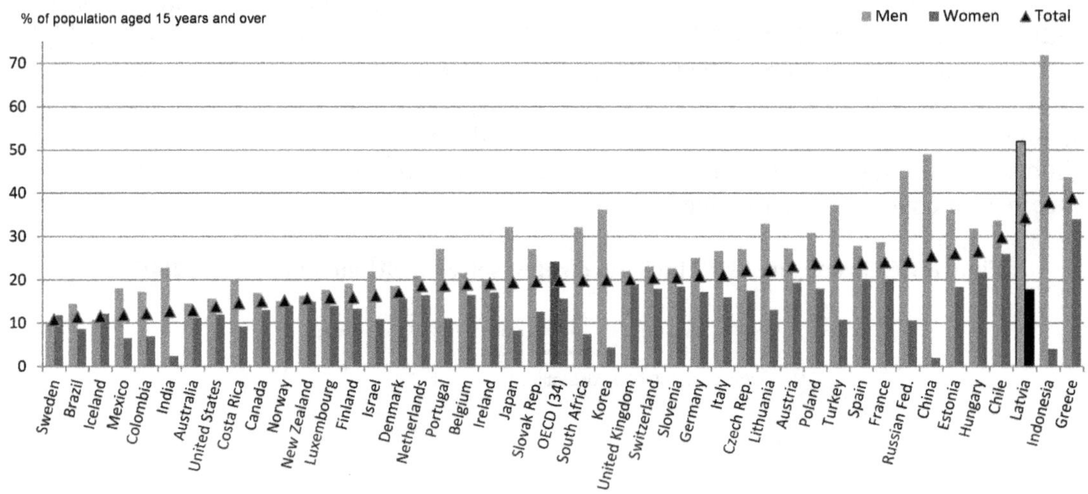

Source: OECD Health Statistics 2015, http://dx.doi.org/10.1787/health-data-en.

The prevalence of other key risk factors is also increasing. Latvian adults consumed 10.3 litres of alcohol per capita in 2012, an increase from 7.1 in 2000. In contrast, OECD countries on average reported a downward trend in alcohol consumption, from 9.5 litres per capita in 2000 to 8.8 in 2013 (OECD, 2015e). It has been estimated that as many as one in eight Latvian adults may have some form of alcohol dependency (CDPC, 2012). These worrying trends may be due to the fact that the price of alcohol did not increase as fast as income in recent years.

The prevalence of obesity is also slightly higher in Latvia at 20.6%, compared to the OECD average of 19.0% (OECD, 2015e). Although many OECD countries report more obesity in men compared to women, in Latvia the obesity rate is higher among women is 25%, compared to 16% among men (CDPC, 2015).

Despite these challenging risk factors, spending on prevention in Latvia is much lower than in many OECD countries. Prevention represents less than 1% of current health spending (equivalent to USD PPP 8.8 per person) compared to the OECD average of 3% (equivalent to just over USD PPP 100 per capita, OECD, 2015e). Investment in public health and prevention is heavily reliant upon the funding from the international community, including the European Union. This has fluctuated somewhat in recent years, so more national resources need to be allocated to this important area in a stable manner.

The increasing prevalence of risk factors and low spending on prevention may be due to the low policy priority given to prevention and promotion of healthy life styles, weak role of primary care in prevention (Chapter 3), and the low level of public awareness on the importance of healthy life styles. Latvia has tried to promote healthy life styles through public campaigns, specific activities targeting school children and focused on promotion of healthy nutrition and anti-smoking, physical activities promotion.

Latvia is increasingly emphasising health promotion and prevention as priority areas for health system investment. Recently, considerable financial resources have been made available for health promotion and prevention activities for years up to 2020. In addition, the Public Health Strategy for 2014-20 lays out to implement a number of activities to strengthen the role of primary health care professionals in health promotion and prevention.

Self-reported health status is low

International comparisons of self-reported data on health status are often difficult to compare because they can be affected by social and cultural factors. Given the high burden of diseases and high prevalence of adverse risk factors in Latvia compared to OECD countries, poor health reported by the population is very likely to signal poor health status in reality (Figure 1.8).

Figure 1.8. Perceived health status among adults, 2013 (or nearest year)

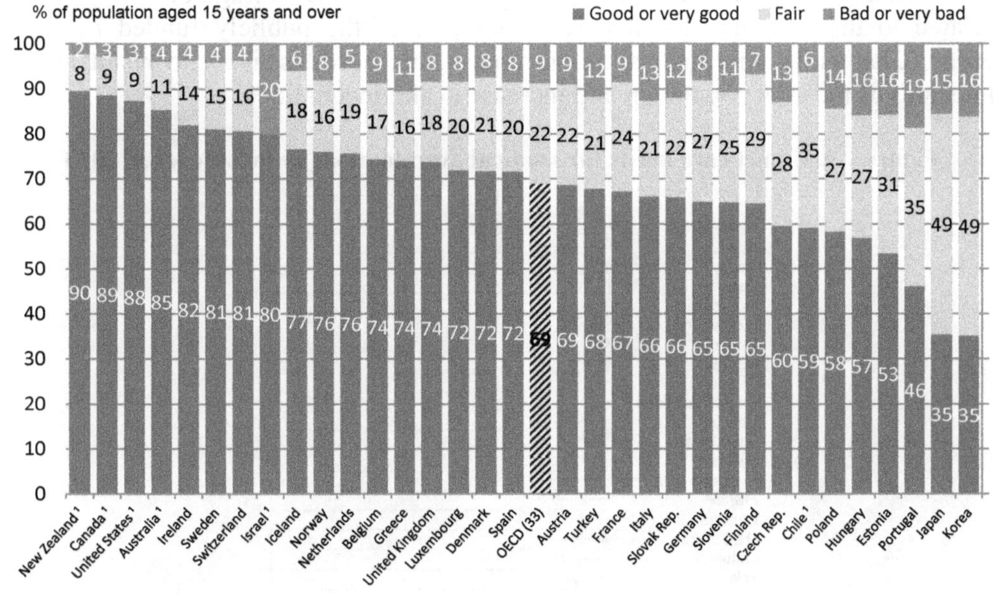

1. Results for these countries are not directly comparable with those for other countries, due to methodological differences in the survey questionnaire resulting in an upward bias. In Israel, there is no category related to fair health.

Source: OECD Health Statistics 2015, http://dx.doi.org/10.1787/health-data-en (EU-SILC for European countries).

More people report poor health status, long-standing illness or limitations in usual activities in Latvia than other OECD countries. Across OECD countries, 69% on average reported to be in good or very good health in 2013. In Latvia, by contrast, the rate was much lower at 37%. The proportion of people reported bad or very bad health was higher in Latvia at 22%, compared to the OECD average of 9%. Self-reported long-standing illness or limitations in usual activities are also higher than many other European countries. For example, 39.7% of Latvians reported having long-standing illness, compared to the European average of 32.5% (Eurostat, 2015). Poor health status reported by the population may reflect not only the high prevalence of communicable and non-communicable diseases and risk factors but also high unmet health care needs (see below and Chapter 2) in Latvia.

Inequalities in health and access to health care are high

The share of Latvian population in higher income groups who reported to be in good health, at 63.1%, is low compared with the OECD average of 79.1%. In lower income groups, only 36.9% report to be in good health, much lower than the OECD average of 61.6% (Eurostat, 2015; OECD, 2015b). The share of low income population with self-perceived longstanding illness is also much higher in Latvia at 43.9% than the European average of 32.7% while the share among high income group is 22.0% in Latvia, compared with the European average of 18.3% (Eurostat, 2015).

Unmet need for health care also shows marked income inequality in Latvia. Among higher income groups, 4.3% report going without needed health care (due to cost, travelling distance or waiting times), compared an OECD average of 1.3% (Figure 1.9).. One quarter of the low income population in Latvia reported going without health care when needed; compared to 5.1% OECD average. Inequality in unmet care needs is even more pronounced in relation to dental examination: 35.8% of the low income group forewent needed care in Latvia, much higher than the OECD average of 9.6%. This may be related to the fact that dental care is not part of the publicly funded health care coverage (Chapter 2). Any inequalities in unmet care needs is likely to result in poorer health status of the total population and increase health inequalities.

Figure 1.9. Unmet care needs for medical examination, by income level, 2013

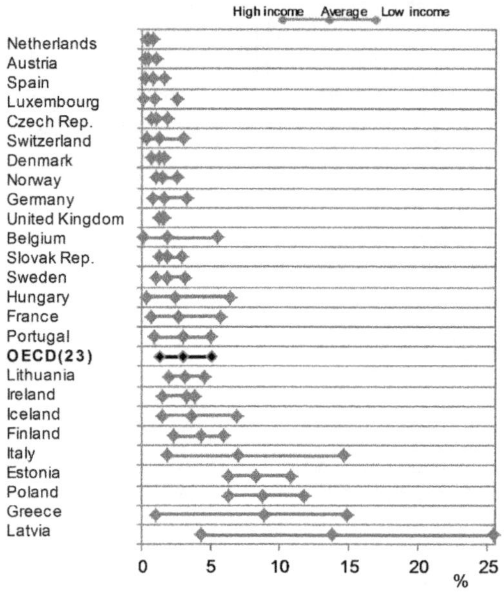

Note: Unmet care needs for following reasons: too expensive, too far to travel, or waiting time.

Source: EU-SILC 2013.

This high health inequality is likely to be associated with high income inequality, which is high in Latvia compared to most other EU countries. Based on the Gini coefficient, the commonly used indicator to examine income inequality, Latvia has the second highest income inequality after Lithuania in the European Union (European Union, 2013). The share of population at risk of poverty or social exclusion is over 35%, more than 10 percentage points higher than the EU average (OECD, 2015d).

1.2. The health system in Latvia

Latvia has undergone a number of system-wide health care reforms since independence. Most importantly, it has developed a single-purchaser national health system, funded by general tax revenues. This offers universal health insurance coverage and access to a relatively full range of basic and specialist health care services. There is a purchaser-provider split, and both public and private providers practice in the health system. Quality assurance mechanisms focus on assuring safety, and the health information infrastructure is developing. This section describes different stakeholders and their role in the Latvian health system and main challenges that they are facing.

Health system governance is largely centralised

Since independence in 1991, public governance in Latvia has evolved continuously, at times emphasising decentralisation of functions, at other times pursuing recentralisation. Immediately post-independence, a shift toward decentralisation created 119 municipalities. These were intended to manage health care plans and drive implementations at the local level, although many of them had a population of less than 2 000. After about a decade, it was concluded that the decentralised system was not appropriate for a small country with a population of around 2 million, and the country shifted the system back to more centralised governance while leaving some limited decision-making authorities at the local level.

At central level, the Parliament, the Cabinet of Ministers and the Ministry of Health (MoH) are the key players in the governance of the Latvian health system. Parliament approves the budget for National Health Service (NHS) and issues the main normative acts and regulations for the health system. Parliament's Health Subcommittee (within the Social and Employment Committee) reviews selected issues raised by its members, other members of Parliament, the MoH, the Directorate of NHS, patient and professional organisations, and other non-governmental organisations. The MoH has responsibility for purchasing health services (see below), and takes charge of the overall organisation and functioning of health systems, designing and implementing specific measures related to priority policy areas.

Other ministries also play important roles in the health system. The Ministry of Welfare is responsible for long-term care and social security, including rehabilitative and nursing care for the disabled, prevention of violence, and ageing issues. The Ministry of Education and Science deals with health promotion activities for school children, including integrated health education to improve health literacy among pupils. It is also responsible for sports policy and medical schools. The Ministry of Agriculture provides programmes to promote healthy food among school children, develops nutrition guidelines and deals with food safety issues.

A number of mergers took place among institutions at the national level until 2011 and state functions were consolidated into five institutions. Two of these relate to specific health care areas, namely the Centre for Disease Prevention and Control for prevention, and the State Emergency Medical Service, both described further below. One is the central purchaser (or NHS, described further below). Finally, two agencies focus on quality assurance – the Health Inspectorate and the State Agency for Medicine. Both are described further in Chapter 2.

The Centre for Disease Prevention and Control (CDPC) is the national public health institute, responsible for collecting, analysing and reporting health information, managing disease registries, implementing public health activities and monitoring disease outbreaks and public health programmes. Its activities are governed by the policies and regulations decided by MoH. In particular, the CDPC regulates public health activities and co-ordinates activities undertaken at local level in the area of health promotion and disease prevention. CDPC manages the National Healthy Municipalities' Network and works together with municipalities to implement prevention and health promotion activities based on the local needs. It develops recommendations and guidelines on prevention and health promotion, as well as training and workshops for health promotion co-ordinators working at the municipality level. In January 2015, the CDPC initiated a Network of Health Promoting Schools. Although some activities are funded by the MoH, EU funds are crucial for CDPC activities. This has led to some concerns regarding the sustainability of health promotion and prevention activities in Latvia.

The State Emergency Medical Service (SEMS) was set up in 2009. It organises emergency care throughout Latvia. It has four specialised units based in hospitals whose role is to co-ordinate the ambulances spread out in the country, and advise on the most appropriate transfer for each patient. The SEMS also has a strategic function, and analyses information such as frequency of ambulance transfers to hospitals and transport time by patient's diagnosis, to identify ways to increase efficiency in delivering emergency care. The quality of emergency care is reported to have improved since the creation of SEMS, as described further in Section 1.3.

Municipalities' main responsibilities are centred on health promotion and prevention, as well as the provision of long-term care services. Municipalities are also expected to assure access to health services by providing subsidies to cover transportation costs to health care facilities for those who need it. They are supported by CDPC in developing activities such as information campaigns related to cardiovascular disease, cancer, reproductive health, and risk factors such as tobacco consumption and lack of physical activity. Many municipalities have health promotion co-ordinators, who are often teachers or social workers. These offer community workshops based on CDPC material. In addition, centres offering counselling, rapid testing and syringe exchange have been established to improve HIV/AIDS prevention.

Revenue collection depends on general taxes, with external assistance playing an important role

The Latvian health system is funded mainly through general taxation collected by the Ministry of Finance. For a few years after the independence in the early 1990s, 28.4% of income tax revenue was earmarked for health and an additional state subsidy funded through general tax was available for health. In 2005, however, this earmarking was abolished. Nowadays, Parliament approves the budget for the NHS (see below). As a result, the health system has to compete with other national policy priorities, leading to a relatively under-funded system by international standards. In order to increase the overall government budget for Latvia, its tax system would also benefit from more efficient revenue collection (OECD, 2015d).

Private insurance plays a modest role in the Latvian health system. There are approximately ten private health insurance companies providing complementary and/or duplicate coverage to about 20% of the population. The share of private insurance market has not changed for over a decade. In 2014, insurance companies collected premiums worth EUR 55 million, which is equivalent to about 4% of current health expenditure. The scope of health care coverage in most insurance schemes is similar, usually covering dental care, medications, laboratory services, optical care and sport clubs. They may also reimburse the costs of seeing non-NHS providers. About 30% of the schemes have different coverage, leading to some level of competition in the market. In the aftermath of the global financial crisis, some insurance schemes excluded coverage of medications that were not reimbursed by NHS, but the extent of coverage for outpatient and inpatient care was generally maintained. Private health insurance is mainly used by a few large companies to make employment contracts more attractive – almost all the privately insured are employees of these companies. Local governments and other public entities also offer private health insurance to their employees, but the coverage of benefits typically more limited.

Latvia's health system receives substantial financial support from the international community. The European Union, for instance, provided EUR 250 million for improving health system infrastructure and EUR 60 million for human resource projects over seven years up to 2013. The EU's current investment, funded until 2020, focuses on cardiovascular diseases, oncology and perinatal and neonatal and mental health through provision of health service as well as health promotion and prevention activities. The World Bank also provides credits to develop Latvia's health system, by investing in ambulatory care and emergency services, training professionals (particularly in primary care) and other activities.

There is no regional tax in Latvia, hence municipalities rely on the central government's revenue for their activities. On average, half the budget is programme-based (linked to initiatives for children and elderly, for example), and half comes through the equalisation system based on the number of population in the municipality.

In Latvia, the patient plays an important role in financing the health system. Out-of-pocket payments account for 38% of total health expenditure in Latvia, double the OECD average of 19% (Figure 1.10). Exemptions for out-of-pocket payment are available for the poor but these are not extensive, leaving many vulnerable populations without access to needed health care (described in more detail in Chapter 2). Municipalities cover some transport cost for certain patients such as diabetes, but some patients do not take up these subsidies.

Figure 1.10. Expenditure on health by type of financing, 2013 (or nearest year)

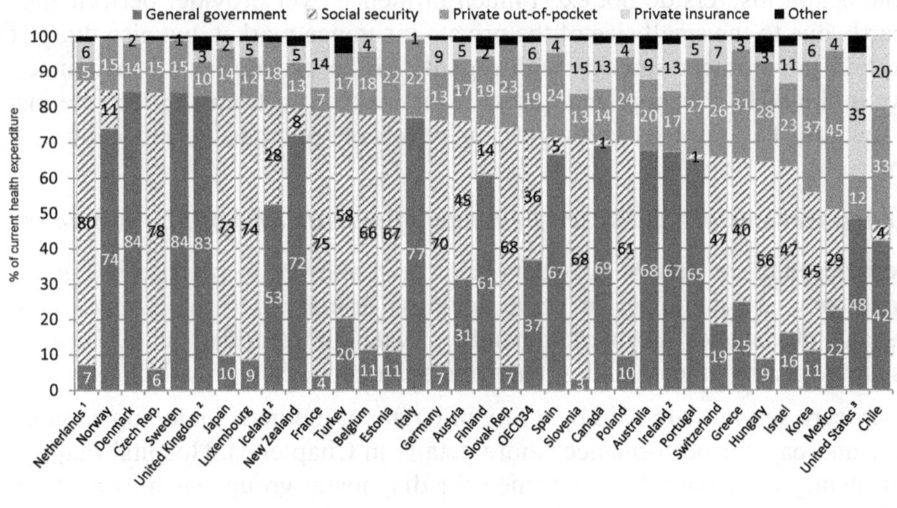

1. The Netherlands report compulsory cost sharing in health care insurance and in Exceptional Medical Expenses Act under social security rather than under private out-of-pocket, resulting in an underestimation of the out-of-pocket share.

2. Data refer to total health expenditure (= current health expenditure plus capital formation).

3. Social security reported together with general government.

Source: OECD Health Statistics 2015, http://dx.doi.org/10.1787/health-data-en.

The single purchaser has played a relatively limited role in improving health system efficiency thus far

Since independence in 1991, the purchaser of health care services has changed several times. For a few years after the independence, Latvia introduced a decentralised social health insurance, leading to numerous regional sickness funds at local level. This did not lead to efficiency gains. Over the following decade, mergers took place and in 2011 a single National Health Service (NHS) was created. This acts as a single purchaser, receiving funds from the MoH and purchasing services from local and national providers. As discussed in Chapter 2, there is scope for the NHS to play a larger role in monitoring and improving health system performance, through selective purchasing and evaluation of providers.

Other main tasks that NHS carries out include deciding coverage and tariffs. The coverage of services reimbursed by NHS is decided based on health technology assessment, which evaluates affordability and cost efficiency for pharmaceutical goods. The scope of NHS coverage is more limited than in other OECD health systems. For instance, some procedures such as thrombolysis for ischemic stroke are excluded. The coverage was reduced in the aftermath of global financial crisis in 2008 in order to contain health spending.

Importantly, the NHS also sets annual quotas for some health care services. These limit access by requiring users to pay the full cost of care out-of-pocket, or through private health insurance, if services exceed the annual threshold, or requiring users to wait for the following year with the renewed quota. Service providers aim to offer care based on the annual quota, but cannot always keep to the threshold, particularly for patients requiring emergency care. The NHS monitors patients' direct payments, and if providers are found deliberately deferring treatment to receive direct payment, the NHS can terminate their contract. Finally, the NHS also manages and develops the e-health system which will be introduced in 2016. This is expected to increase efficiencies in the health system.

Private health insurers do not exert much influence over provider performance either. This is partly due to the small size of the private insurance market, but also due to the lack of an explicit government strategy with regards to the private health insurance market, instability in the NHS coverage and quotas. This makes it difficult for private insurers to develop medium to long-term strategies on coverage, purchasing and contracting with providers.

Health care services are delivered by a mix of private and public providers

Since independence, private providers have been allowed to practice in Latvian health system and they are dominant in some settings. Primary care physicians, dental care providers and pharmacies are predominantly private. In secondary care, however, most hospitals are owned by municipalities, but some ambulatory care providers are private.

Primary care services are paid by a mix of payment methods including capitation, fee-for-service and pay-for-performance (more details in Chapter 3). Hospital outpatient care is funded mainly by a flat rate determined for diagnostic groups such as acute diseases, chronic diseases and prevention, and fee-for-service payments. Inpatient care used to be paid through fee-for-service up to a specific upper limit but after several years of a transitional period with quasi-diagnosis-related group (DRG) payment system, a full-fledged DRG system was introduced in 2015.

There are three types of public ownership for hospitals, and they abide by different financial obligations. Although Latvia is a small country, municipalities own most of the 30 hospitals in the country. Each municipality makes its own procurement and capital investment decisions, resulting in a large numbers of expensive pieces of equipment, such as MRI scanners (discussed further in Chapter 2).

Central government owns several tertiary and specialised hospitals. In contrast to municipality-owned hospitals, these are under more restrictive financing obligations, and also pay dividends to the central government. There are also a few state-owned enterprises including three university hospitals, three psychiatric hospitals, three orthopaedic hospitals and three emergency hospitals, for which the majority of the budget comes from the state. They are not allowed to be at loss at the end of the fiscal year. Given the diversity of these arrangements, the organisation of secondary and tertiary care could benefit from a national strategic plan, similar to that achieved for emergency care, in order to reduce inefficiencies.

Professional associations are responsible for assuring professional quality

Several professional associations represent the interest of health care practitioners in Latvia. The Pharmacist's Society of Latvia is the largest health professional association and more than one-third of pharmacists are its members. The Latvian Medical Association (LMA) is an umbrella organisation for 109 associations representing different medical specialties. The Latvian Nurses Association (LNA) has about half of professional nurses as its members.

These associations give professional certifications and keep registers of professionals. For example, the LMA gives professional certification and re-certification to specialists. Re-certification is given every five years with 250 hours of training, otherwise physicians need to take a relicensing exam. Similarly, the LNA certifies and recertifies nurses.

Latvia has a well-developed health system information infrastructure

The CDPC has principal responsibility to collect and report health system information relating to public health, prevention and quality of care. It manages both administrative databases and a number of registries including those for cancer, mental health, diabetes, tuberculosis, and occupational health which have been created since the late 1990s. Data from private providers are not usually included, which is of some concern particularly for mental health because the private sector plays a significant role in care provision. CDPC also analyses registry data together with NHS data to evaluate prescription patterns. Doctors receive standardised reports to compare their performance against national averages in terms of clinical measures, treatment and complications. Most data are available in the public domain, sometimes disaggregated by region, but not by provider.

Other public agencies are also involved in national health system monitoring. The NHS manages data reported from providers in primary care and secondary care on activities and expenditures. On its website, it reports hospital data such as average length of stay (ALOS), use of hospital and observation beds, and hospital admission rates. The NHS also reports waiting times, although this is not always considered up-to-date. The Central Bureau of Statistics also provides health expenditure data and conducts surveys such as the Health Interview Survey and Labour Force Survey (which includes health workforce data), the European Health Survey for Disability and the Survey on Income and Living Conditions (SILC) which measures unmet care needs among others. Finally, the Health Inspectorate regularly reports information related to inspection results.

Overall, Latvia has good health system data, allowing it to be included in the OECD's Health Statistics and benchmarked alongside other OECD countries (OECD, 2014b; OECD, 2015b). Latvia also participates in Baltic report, published every four years, comparing health system performance among Baltic and Nordic countries. Nonetheless, more can be done to develop data-driven health planning and governance in Latvia, as discussed further in Chapter 2.

Introduction of e-health provides an opportunity to improve both quality and efficiency

Latvia has been strengthening its health information infrastructure in recent years and, with the step-wise introduction of an e-health system started in 2015, the availability and use of health information should increase further. All providers including GPs, hospitals and pharmacies and patients will participate in e-health in which they can share data on patients including their diagnoses, health care services received such as diagnosis and treatment and medication prescribed and purchased. It is anticipated that patients will use a card containing their unique patient ID to pay for all health services and medications, allowing their health care utilisation data to be collected. Providers will need to provide information about patients including their diagnoses, treatment provided and medication prescribed in order to get reimbursed by NHS and this will be linked with the utilisation data in the e-health system.

It is planned that the information provided from these sources will be integrated into a comprehensive single data warehouse. The system should allow access to health information via the internet, allowing patients to engage more in taking control of their own health conditions. Provider coverage is initially limited, but envisaged to cover all providers in future years. Of note, Latvia has been working closely with Estonia to learn from their experiences in introducing e-health system.

Introduction of the e-health system is expected to increase the quality of health care as well as system efficiency. For instance, health care providers can issue e-prescriptions so that patients can purchase medications in any pharmacy in the country, and this will enable providers to monitor medication safety when multiple drugs are prescribed for patients. Likewise, co-ordination across providers is expected to improve by avoiding, for example, duplicated diagnostic tests and informing GPs when their patient is discharged from hospital.

Patient voice is somewhat limited and there is significant room to increase population health literacy

A number of patient organisations have been found since the 1990s for patients with specific diseases such as diabetes and lymphoma. Several of these are members of Latvian Umbrella Body for Disability Organisations (SUSTENTO), which represents approximately 50 000 people with illness or disability (Mitenbergs et al., 2012). SUSTENTO takes part in different working groups of MoH and MoW, provides their views in policy issues related to transport, education and science and collaborates with various stakeholders including industry.

Latvia's Patients' Ombudsman Office is a non-governmental organisation, active in providing patients' views on how to improve the Latvian health system and in promoting patients' rights. It conducts research on patient experiences, and collects complaints regarding access and quality of care in both primary care and hospital settings. The Office engages in mediation between professionals and patients where disputes have arisen. It also works to increase public awareness on access and quality, such as improving communication between professionals and patients.

Although information on NHS-funded providers and their services is available publically through websites and hotlines, the extent to which the Latvian population feels enabled to understand and improve their own health remains unclear. For example, Latvia offers free screening for breast and cervical cancer. Screening rates, however, are very low compared to other OECD health systems (see Chapter 3). In addition, although patients have a right to access medical records, many of them do not know about this. The introduction of e-health and public reporting of provider performance could improve the health literacy of the Latvian population if they are well designed and formats are oriented toward the general population, as well as to clinicians and managers.

1.3. Resources in the Latvian health system

The Latvian health system is relatively under-resourced compared to other OECD countries. Just over 5% of GDP is spent on health care, with nearly 40% of this coming from out-of-pocket sources. The country has implemented a number of important reforms, such as consolidation of the hospital sector, to maintain health service delivery despite the challenging financial context. Nevertheless, strains are apparent. The shortage of hospital specialists in rural areas is a particularly pressing example.

Total spending on health is low and public health financing is very low by OECD standards

Latvia spent 5.3% GDP on health care in 2013 (equivalent to USD PPP 1 217 per person per year), substantially lower than the OECD average of 8.9% (equivalent to USD PPP 3 453). This is partly because public health system funding is just 3.2% GDP, half the OECD average of 6.5% in 2013 (Figure 1.11). Among other OECD countries, only Mexico, Chile, Turkey and Korea spend less than 4% of GDP on health through public financing. In contrast, public health funding accounts for more than 8% GDP in Netherlands, Sweden, Denmark, France, Japan and Germany.

Between 2005 and 2009, GDP in Latvia grew on average 2.0% annually in real terms, much faster than 0.6% on average across OECD countries. Health spending, however, only increased by 3.0% annually, less than the OECD average of 3.4%. Between 2009 and 2013, the Latvian recovered more quickly from the financial crisis than other OECD economies, with annual GDP growth of 4.3% on average, compared to the OECD average of 1.1%. Growth in health spending during this period was, however, no different to the OECD average at 0.6% during the same period. Given these figures, it could be argued that Latvia has had more fiscal space to devote to health system investment than other OECD economies.

Latvia allocates a significantly smaller proportion of GDP to the public sector than the European OECD countries and the share of public spending in health is also very small. The proportion of GDP to the public sector in Latvia is 36.5%, much lower than the average of all European OECD countries (excluding Turkey) at 45.6% in 2012 (OECD, 2015d) and Latvia spends 9% of public expenditure in health, a smaller share than any OECD countries (Figure 1.13). At the other end of the spectrum, the share is over 20% in New Zealand, Switzerland, the Netherlands and the United States.

Figure 1.11. Health expenditure as a share of GDP, 2013 (or nearest year)

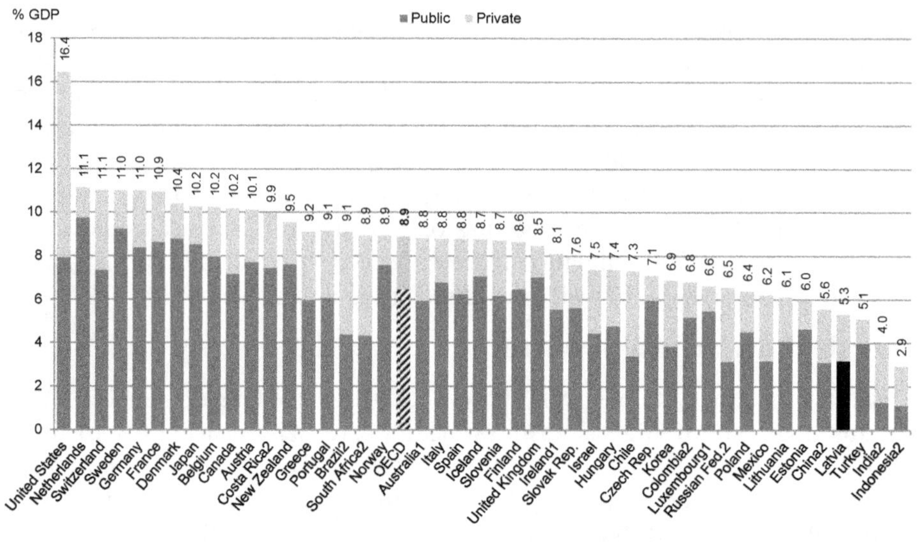

Source: OECD Health Statistics, 2015, http://dx.doi.org/10.1787/health-data-en.

There is some evidence that low levels of spending on health in Latvia is holding it back from achieving the health outcomes that should be expected given its broader economic context. Using life expectancy a proxy, health outcomes are much lower than expected in Latvia Given the level of GDP per capita (Figure 1.12). Chile, Poland and Hungary have higher life expectancies for a similar per capita GDP – and all these countries spend a larger share of GDP on health. This suggests that increasing spending on health should be an option that Latvia considers. Improving health system efficiency will also be critical.

Figure 1.12. Life expectancy at birth and GDP per capita, 2013 (or nearest year)

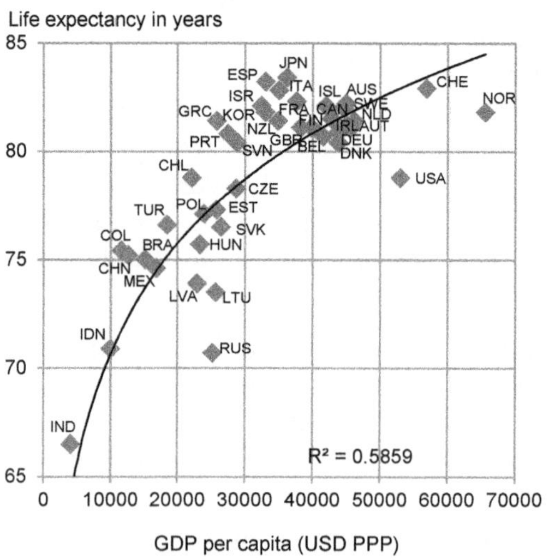

Source: OECD Health Statistics 2015, http://dx.doi.org/10.1787/health-data-en.

Figure 1.13. Health expenditure as a share of public expenditure, 2013 (or nearest year)

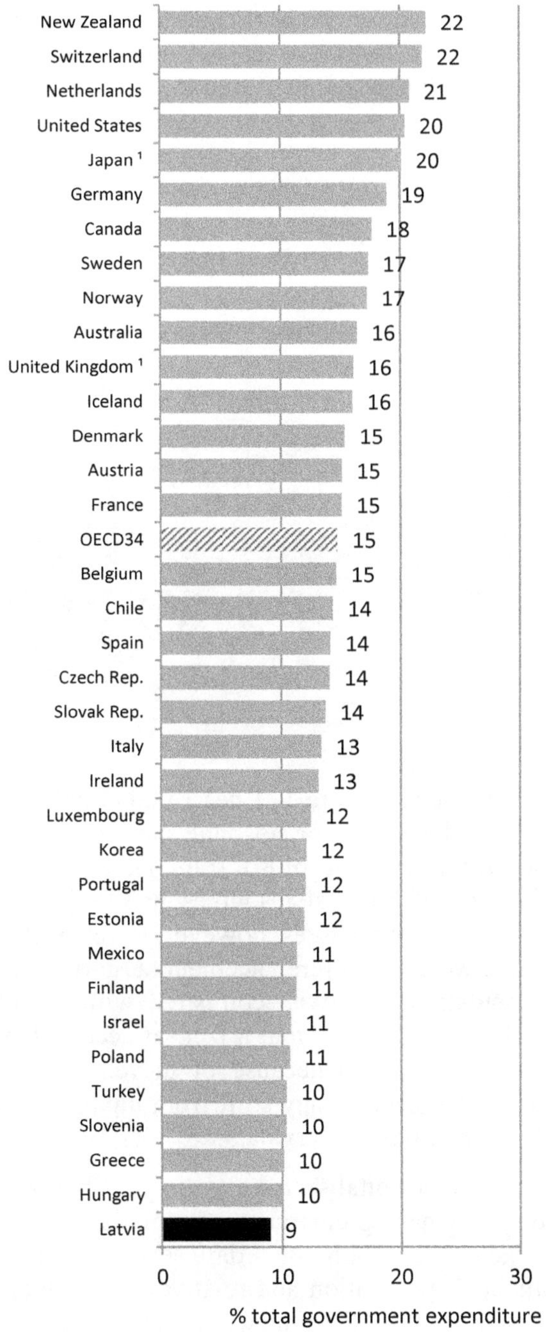

1. Data refer to total health expenditure (= current health expenditure plus capital formation).

Source: OECD Health Statistics 2015, http://dx.doi.org/10.1787/health-data-en; OECD National Accounts; Eurostat Statistics Database; IMF World Economic Outlook Database.

Hospitals have been consolidated in recent years, but elderly care has received less attention

The hospital sector has been significantly consolidated in the past decade, as part of a move to shift from inpatient care to outpatient and home care. The number of hospital beds has fallen from 8.8 per 1 000 population to 5.8, approaching to the OECD average of 4.8 (Figure 1.14).

Figure 1.14. Hospital beds per 1 000 population, 2013 (or nearest year)

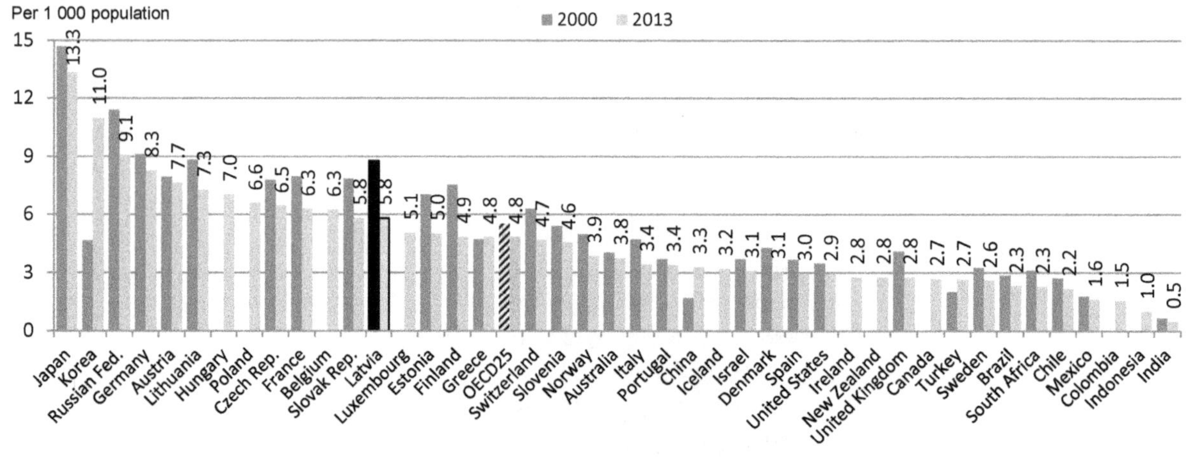

Source: OECD Health Statistics 2015, http://dx.doi.org/10.1787/health-data-en.

The number of hospital discharges are 172 per 1 000 population, slightly higher than the OECD average of 155. The length of hospital stay is 7.6 days on average for all causes, shorter than the OECD average of 8.1 (OECD, 2015e). Both of these figures suggest a more intensive use of hospital resources in Latvia compared to the OECD average. The number of inpatient procedures, however, is generally lower than the OECD average. For example, there were 106 hip replacement surgeries and 46 knee replacement surgeries per 100 000 population in Latvia, compared with the OECD average of 161 and 121 respectively in 2013. This may signal a lack of access due to actual services (as opposed to the hospital infrastructure) because of the annual quota system discussed earlier. It is not possible to comment on any shift from inpatient procedures to same-day surgeries due to the lack of same-day surgery data.

Further consolidation in the hospital sector may be possible, while assuring quality of care. For instance, Latvia still has 23 emergency hospitals but all of them do not have capacity to provide emergency care 24 hours a day, seven days a week. This may be too many for a country with small population and relatively easy geographic access. Fewer, better-equipped emergency hospitals, distributed strategically across regions, are may be a better option and this should be modelled.

Given the high health and social care needs among the elderly, Latvia will also need to address access and quality in the long-term care sector. Although population ageing is not progressing as quickly as in many OECD countries, the current share of the population that is elderly is higher than the OECD countries, so care for the elderly needs to be an important policy priority for Latvia. However, the number of long-term care beds is lower than most OECD countries (Figure 1.15). Due to the lack of beds, hospitals are also used to care for some elderly who need help with their daily activities. Hospital care is not the most cost-effective way of providing LTC, nor the most pleasant for the patient, compared to a dedicated nursing or residential facility. In general, more facilities providing high quality LTC and nursing care are needed across municipalities in Latvia.

Figure 1.15. Long-term care beds in institutions and hospitals, 2013 (or nearest year)

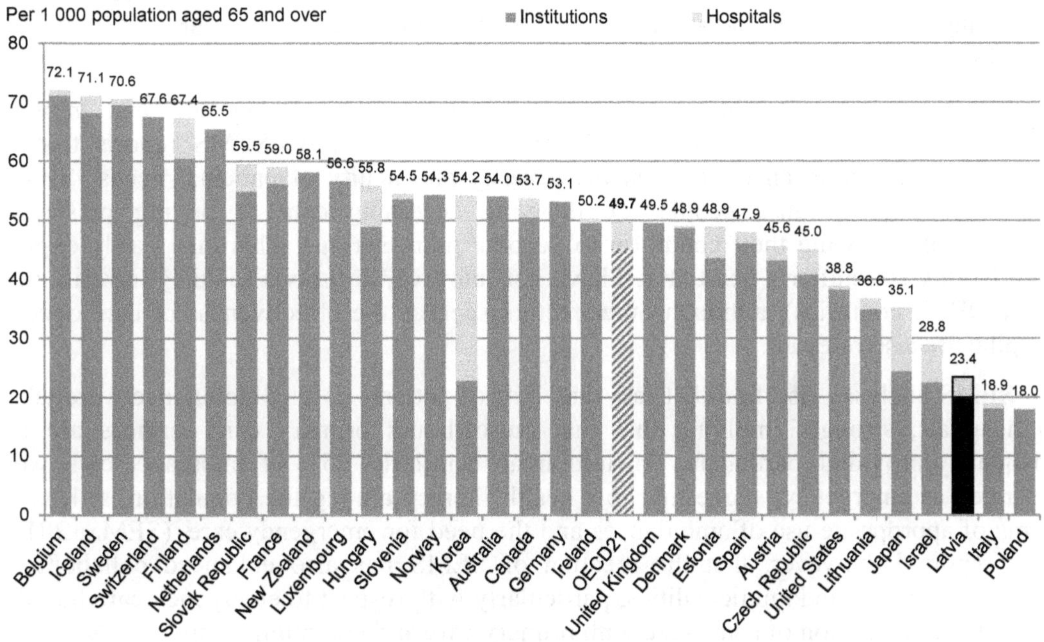

Source: OECD Health Statistics 2015, http://dx.doi.org/10.1787/health-data-en.

The NHS has started to reimburse home care since 2009. GPs and nurses in primary care and hospital now provide a range of home care services for the elderly, and others such as cancer patients and children with complex care needs. However, as in other OECD countries, family support continues to play a significant role in caring for patients needing care at home. Some OECD countries provide respite care and/or allowances for these informal carers (Colombo et al., 2011) but these forms of support are still not well developed in Latvia.

Latvia's emergency care system has been reorganised to increase its accessibility and efficiency

To assure fast access to acute care, the State Emergency Medical Service (SEMS) was introduced in 2009. SEMS is a centralised system that co-ordinates the transport patients to emergency care facilities, using a standardised triage system. There is a transfer time limit of four hours and SEMS monitors a number of performance indicators linked to this. Emergency care units in hospitals, mainly those in big cities, consult with ambulance teams to identify the appropriate hospitals for transfer and if needed, doctors are sent from large cities to care for patients coming from other regions. Emergency care is provided based on guidelines, and the compliance to guidelines is monitored. Failure to comply can trigger financial or other penalties, based on assessment by a Special Commission set up to maintain and improve the quality of the SEMS service.

SEMS has been associated with reduced transfer times to emergency care facilities, despite reduction in the number of hospitals providing emergency care and subsequent increase in distances. Although this is a promising achievement, it does not yet appear to be reflected in key indicators of the quality of acute care. Fatality rates following a heart attack show an show a worsening picture, with patient-based 30-day case-fatality increasing from 17.5 per 100 admissions of adults aged 45 years and over in 2008 to 19.2 in 2013 (OECD, 2015e)

SEMS records all contacts, and uses this information to monitor and improve performance across the Latvian health system more broadly. SEMS reports that its analyses demonstrate an increase in the severity and acuity of patients' needs (SEMS, 2014), possibly because people are delaying accessing care or buying prescribed medications, allowing their condition to become more serious. This may partly explain why fatality rates after a heart attack have not improved in Latvia (as they have in most other OECD countries), although other factors such as the effectiveness of care once in hospital are also relevant.

SEMS analyses also find that less than half of patients calling ambulance were taken to hospitals, strongly implying that that out-of-hours primary care services are not adequately provided, particularly in rural areas. Similarly, 25% of ambulance calls were not rated as emergency, suggesting low health literacy among the population, at least in terms of appropriate use of ambulances and the need for emergency care, (SEMS, 2014). It is reported, however, that the creation of SEMS has also enhanced collaboration between hospitals and municipalities, particularly with respect to emergency care but also in terms of integration of acute care with primary care and community care.

The data and analyses produced by SEMS have potentially great value in improving performance of the health system more broadly. Emergency services need to provide care even if annual quotas for specific services are already filled, for example, so the number of such cases can provide some indication of whether quotas are appropriately set. The origin and ultimate destination of patients can also provide an indication of whether capacity in various levels of care is adequate, both in terms of access and quality of care.

Shortages of some key health professionals are anticipated

Shortages of some professional groups in the health care workforce are anticipated. In 2013, there were 3.1 practicing doctors per 1 000 population, close to the OECD average of 3.2, and a slight increase from 2000 when there were 2.9 practicing doctors per 1 000 population in Latvia. Of note, though, many doctors are expected to retire in coming years.

In contrast, the number of practicing nurses is relatively low at 4.9 per 1 000 population, compared with the OECD average of 9.1 (Figure 1.16). In 2000, there were 4.6 nurses per 1 000 population in Latvia, hence despite the challenge of emigration, discussed earlier, the nursing workforce has been held broadly stable. The ratio of nurses to physicians is low, however, at 1.5 (compared to the OECD average of 2.8). As with doctors, the average age of nurses and other supporting professionals is also increasing, making it challenging to secure their future supply. Currently, doctor assistants, who are trained in emergency and outpatient care for diagnosis and prescribing, play a role between doctors and nurses, filling the resource gap particularly in rural areas.

Figure 1.16. Practising nurses per 1 000 population, 2013 (or nearest year)

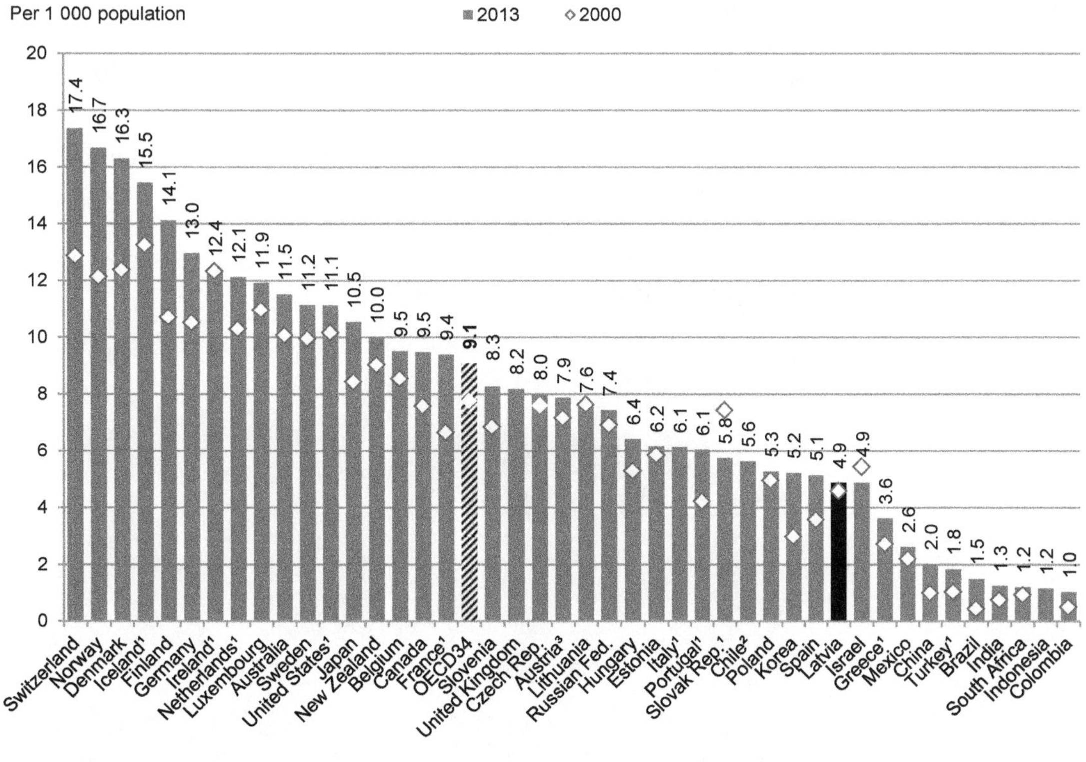

1. Data include not only nurses providing direct care to patients, but also those working in the health sector as managers, educators, researchers, etc.

2. Data refer to all nurses who are licensed to practice.

3. Austria reports only nurses employed in hospital.

Source: OECD Health Statistics 2013, http://dx.doi.org/10.1787/health-data-en.

There are more secondary care specialists in Latvia, 2.5 per 1 000 population, than the OECD average of 2.0. The number of primary care physicians, however, is low at 0.7 per 1 000 population, compared to 1.0 OECD average. Specialists are concentrated in large cities and shortages are a particularly pressing issue in rural areas. Shortages in emergency medical specialists, anaesthetists, intensive care specialists and ophthalmologists are reportedly particularly pressing in rural areas. Rural municipalities have tried a number of initiatives to attract specialists, including salary supplements and free accommodation. Shortages persist, however, signaling a complex problem that is likely to need additional initiatives (such as improvements to rural schooling and other services) to attract health professionals and their families.

Latvian medical and nursing graduates are considered well-trained and they sometimes seek employment opportunities elsewhere in Europe, such as in Germany, Norway and the United Kingdom. The demand for specialised nurses, such as surgical nurses and intensive care nurses, is particularly high in Europe, leading to a relatively high expatriation rate for nurses at 5.0%, as discussed earlier (OECD, 2015c).

It is challenging to assure an adequate supply of nurses in Latvia also because people who have trained as a nurse do not necessarily choose to practice nursing care. This is driven both by difficult working conditions in the health system, as well as opportunities in other sectors, such as private health and well-being centres. Although many returned to work in nursing following the 2008 global financial crisis (as it offered more stable employment compared with other sectors affected by the economic downturn), on average about 150 nurses choose to discontinue to work as nurses while about 200 to 350 nurses are trained every year.

Recently, there have been efforts to increase nurses in primary care. A number of nurses have moved from hospital to provide primary care due to improvements in pay. This increased the number of nurses in primary care but exacerbated shortages in the hospital sector. More comprehensive human resource strategies need to be taken to assure adequate supply of different professionals across all care sectors.

References

CDPC – Centre for Disease Prevention and Control (2012), Atkaribu_izraisoso_vielu_lietosanas_izplatiba_un_sekas_Latvija_2011_gada%20(6).pdf, p. 39.

Colombo, F. et al. (2011), *Help Wanted? Providing and Paying for Long-Term Care*, OECD Health Policy Studies, OECD Publishing, Paris, http://dx.doi.org/10.1787/9789264097759-en.

ECDC and WHO Regional Office for Europe (2013), *HIV/AIDS Surveillance in Europe 2012.*

European Union (2013), *Health Inequalities in the EU – Final Report of a Consortium,* consortium lead: Sir Michael Marmot.

Eurostat Database (2015), http://ec.europa.eu/eurostat/data/database.

EU-SILC (2013), http://ec.europa.eu/eurostat/statistics-explained/index.php/Glossary:EU_statistics_on_income_and_living_conditions_(EU-SILC)/fr.

Hazans, M. (2011), "Labour Market Integration in Latvia", in M. Kahanec and K.F. Zimmermann (eds.), *Ethnic Diversity in European Labour Markets*, Edward Elgar Publishing.

IARC – International Agency for Research on Cancer (2015), *Country Factsheets: Latvia*, http://eu-cancer.iarc.fr/eucan/Country.aspx?ISOCountryCd=428.

Mitenbergs, U.et al. (2012), "Latvia: Health System Review". *Health Systems in Transition*, Vol. 14, No. 8, pp. 1-191.

OECD (2015a), *Cardiovascular Disease and Diabetes: Policies for Better Health and Quality of Care*, OECD Health Policy Studies, OECD Publishing, Paris, http://dx.doi.org/10.1787/9789264233010-en.

OECD (2015b), *Health at a Glance 2015: OECD Indicators*, OECD Publishing, Paris, http://dx.doi.org/10.1787/health_glance-2015-en.

OECD (2015c), *International Migration Outlook 2015*, OECD Publishing, Paris, http://dx.doi.org/10.1787/migr_outlook-2015-en.

OECD (2015d), *OECD Economic Surveys: Latvia 2015*, OECD Publishing, Paris, http://dx.doi.org/10.1787/9789264228467-en.

OECD (2015e), *OECD Health Statistics 2015*, http://dx.doi.org/10.1787/health-data-en.

OECD (2015f), *OECD Reviews of Health Care Quality: Portugal 2015: Raising Standards*, OECD Publishing, Paris, http://dx.doi.org/10.1787/9789264225985-en.

OECD (2015g), *Tackling Harmful Alcohol Use: Economics and Public Health Policy*, OECD Publishing, Paris, http//dx.doi.org/10.1787/9789264181069-en.

OECD (2014a), *Cancer Care: Assuring Quality to Improve Survival*, OECD Health Policy Studies, OECD Publishing, Paris, http://dx.doi.org/10.1787/9789264181052-en.

OECD (2014b), *Health at a Glance: Europe 2014*, OECD Publishing, Paris, http://dx.doi.org/10.1787/health_glance_eur-2014-en.

OECD (2014c), *Making Mental Health Count: The Social and Economic Costs of Neglecting Mental Health Care*, OECD Health Policy Studies, OECD Publishing, Paris, http://dx.doi.org/10.1787/9789264208445-en.

OECD (2013a), *Cancer Care: Assuring Quality to Improve Survival*, OECD Health Policy Studies, OECD Publishing, Paris, http://dx.doi.org/10.1787/9789264181052-en.

OECD (2013b), *International Migration Outlook 2013*, OECD Publishing, Paris, http://dx.doi.org/10.1787/migr_outlook-2013-en.

OECD (2013c), *OECD Reviews of Health Care Quality: Denmark 2013: Raising Standards*, OECD Publishing, Paris, http://dx.doi.org/10.1787/9789264191136-en.

Sassi, F. (2010), *Obesity and the Economics of Prevention: Fit Not Fat*, OECD Publishing, Paris, http://dx.doi.org/10.1787/9789264084865-en.

Schell, C.O. et al. (2007), "Socioeconomic Determinants of Infant Mortality: A Worldwide Study of 152 Low-, Middle-, and High-income Countries", *Scandinavian Journal of Public Health*, Vol. 35, pp. 288-297.

SEMS – State Emergency Medical Service (2014), *State Emergency Medical Service of Latvia (SEMS)*, Riga.

WHO Global Youth Tobacco Survey (forthcoming), WHO, Geneva.

Chapter 2

Performance of the Latvian health system

This chapter assesses the Latvian health system's performance across four domains: access, quality, efficiency and sustainability. Overall, the health system in Latvia is performing well. Despite challenging economic circumstances, in the past five years Latvia has delivered significant reforms to the hospital sector, closing a number of hospitals and 18 emergency departments in a drive to improve efficiency.

Nonetheless, there are some causes for concern, some room for improvement, and some missed opportunities to better exploit existing resources. Accessibility, both economic and geographical, is a major concern, with out-of-pocket payments remain high. Poor performance on some indicators of health care quality are also worrying. The chapter makes recommendations for improvement, drawing on best-practice examples from OECD countries. Where Latvia has implemented innovative reforms, these are highlighted so that OECD countries might learn from Latvian experience.

The statistical data for Israel are supplied by and under the responsibility of the relevant Israeli authorities. The use of such data by the OECD is without prejudice to the status of the Golan Heights, East Jerusalem and Israeli settlements in the West Bank under the terms of international law.

Introduction

The health system in Latvia is performing well despite some truly challenging circumstances, particularly around economic resources; Latvia's health budget, already low, was cut significantly following the 2008 economic crisis. Despite this, in the past five years Latvia has managed to make significant reforms to the hospital sector, closing a number of hospitals and 18 emergency departments in a reportedly effective drive to improve efficiency.

Nonetheless, there are some causes for concern and missed opportunities to better exploit existing resources. Accessibility, both economic and geographical, is a major concern, with out-of-pocket payments very high. Some indicators of health care quality are also worrying; for example, case fatality after stroke is almost three times higher than the OECD average. As Latvia looks to tackle these and other problems, and drive improvements in the system, the relative lack of resources in the system will undoubtedly be a major challenge.

This chapter provides an assessment of Latvia's performance across the dimensions of access, quality, efficiency and sustainability. A description of the current state of the system, which complements Chapter 1 of this report, is accompanied by an analysis of strengths and weaknesses across these areas. Where appropriate, recommendations for improvement are given, alongside best-practice examples from OECD countries. Where Latvia has taken innovative steps, or made impressive improvements, these are highlighted so that OECD countries might learn from Latvian experience.

2.1. Access to care

Since the establishment of Latvia's National Health System (NHS) in 2011, all Latvians should have access to a growing package of health care services, an equal access to care is a clear policy priority. However, compared to other OECD countries some gaps in coverage are apparent. Additionally, waiting times can be long, and co-payments are high. Many of these challenges are caused by, or exacerbated by, Latvia's "quota" system for health care services.

The Latvian NHS provides a relatively full range of health care services

Since the establishment of Latvia's National Health System in 2011 all Latvian residents should have access to a full range of health care, and equal access to care is a clear policy priority; paragraph 111 of the Latvian Constitution states that "The state shall protect human health and guarantee a basic level of medical assistance for everyone". However, some gaps in service coverage are apparent.

The service package available in the NHS covers services provided by physicians and institutions which have contracted with the NHS. The benefit basket is determined by both "positive lists" (for pharmaceuticals, and for certain diagnostic, preventative and therapeutic interventions under Regulation No. 1046) and negative lists (exclusion of certain services under Regulation No. 1046, including dental care for adults, rehabilitation, sight and hearing correction aids). Family doctors act as gatekeepers (except in case of emergency) for most diagnostic, specialist and hospital services. Without a referral costs must be covered by the patient, either out-of-pocket or by their own health insurance (Mitenbergs et al., 2012).

Cost sharing and out-of-pocket payments are applied across health services, and may constitute a financial barrier to access

The contribution of out-of-pocket spending to total health care expenditure in Latvia is significant, at 38.5% in 2013 (see Chapter 1). OPP medical spending represented 3.4% of final household consumption in Latvia in 2013, above the OECD average of 2.8%, and enough to be understood as a significant barrier to many Latvians. A significant proportion of out-of-pocket payments in Latvia go towards paying for pharmaceuticals (48%); a further 33% of OPPs was spent on curative care.

Part of Latvia's high OPP spend is explained by the cost sharing and out-of-pocket payments which are applied across all Latvian NHS services. Exemptions and annual and/or per-hospital stay caps are, however, in place. Direct payments for services not covered by the NHS (such as dental care, or eyeglasses), or for services without a referral from a GP, or outside of NHS service provision, are common. Paying out of pocket to avoid long waits for services, especially towards the end of the year when NHS service quotas have been exhausted – see discussion of waiting lists, and quotas, which follows – is reported as common.

Latvia had been taking steps to protect households from catastrophic health spending, targeting lower income groups for increased protection under the Safety Net and Social Sector Reform Programme. While some co-payment and co-insurance rates were increased from 2009 (for certain pharmaceuticals, for some specialist care, and an increase in the annual user charge cap), Latvia also introduced a scheme to protect the poorest population groups from financial risk under the "Emergency Social Safety Net Strategy" (see Box 2.1). The scheme was introduced in October 2009, with input from the World Bank. Among broader measures around education and social assistance, the scheme temporarily exempted certain households from health co-payments, and subsidised pharmaceuticals for the poorest households. In 2010 about 21 500 patients were exempted from user charges for pharmaceuticals; co-payments were covered for 23 400 inpatient stays, 42 200 day cases, 129 100 outpatients and 5 800 home care patients (Mitenbergs et al., 2012). However, at the end of the implementation term of the programme, in 2011, the exemption from user charges for low income households was ended.

Box 2.1. The Safety Net and Social Sector Reform Programme

Following the financial crisis the Safety Net and Social Sector Reform Programme introduced a number of measures aimed at improving access, including: 1) free hotel-type accommodation in hospitals for needy and low-income patients from remote areas who would otherwise be unable to travel back home after having received day-care services in hospitals; 2) free home-care services for chronically ill patients to remove financial barriers such as travel expenses and hospitalisation expenses; 3) improved staffing at GP practices by hiring an additional nurse; 4) the introduction of a family physician advisory telephone service to connect patients to a doctor after working hours and at weekends (when family doctor offices are closed); and, 5) the establishment of day centres for mental health to provide services in the community and to better integrate patients in society.

Although the term of implementation of the Strategy ended in 2013, some of the measures of the Strategy were integrated into the basic health budget and continued. This includes measures to improve accessibility to health care services for needy groups, and efforts to develop out-patient services. Exemption from cost sharing for low income groups was not continued. Health care measures building from this programme were also included in the Strategic Development Plan of Latvia for 2010-13 (see Chapter 1, Section 2.4).

Source: Mitenbergs, U. et al. (2012), "Latvia: Health System Review", *Health Systems in Transition*, Vol. 14, No. 8, pp. 1-191.

High levels of cost sharing appear to be presenting a financial barrier to access, and the removal of exemptions for poorer households post-2011 raises further concerns. Health expenditure as a proportion of all household expenditures rose following the financial crisis, having fallen in the run up to 2011, very possibly due to the prior application of exemptions.

The high co-payment for services is still reported by the Minister for Health as stopping some 12-20% of Latvians from accessing health services, and in 2013 was reported by 23.5% of Latvians surveyed as the reason for unmet medical examination (see also Chapter 1). In the 2013 EU-SILC survey, of those surveyed reporting unmet need for medical examination, 23% of Latvian respondents reported that cost ("too expensive") as an explanation (Figure 2.1). Unmet needs for medical examination where cost is a barrier appears to have increased since the financial crisis. In 2007, 2008 and 2009 fewer than 20% of Latvians reported unmet need for care with the reason "too expensive", rising to 25.9% in 2010 and 26.1% in 2011 (EU-SILC, 2013). Latvia was hit particularly hard by the financial crisis, with GDP falling by around a quarter. The impact of the financial crisis on unmet needs for medical examination also appeared more acute in Latvia than in other European countries hit by the crisis, for example Ireland and Portugal, where self-reported unmet need rose slightly from 2009 but mostly stayed below 5%.

Figure 2.1. Self-reported unmet needs for medical examination, 2013

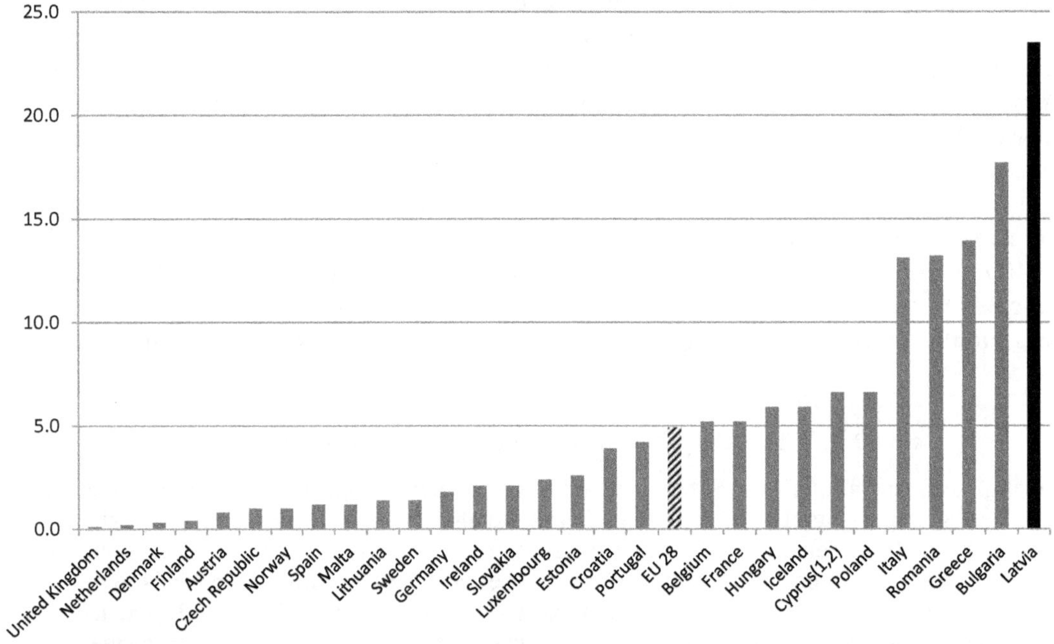

1. *Note by Turkey:* The information in this report with reference to "Cyprus" relates to the southern part of the Island. There is no single authority representing both Turkish and Greek Cypriot people on the Island. Turkey recognises the Turkish Republic of Northern Cyprus (TRNC). Until a lasting and equitable solution is found within the context of the United Nations, Turkey shall preserve its position concerning the "Cyprus issue".

2. *Note by all the European Union Member States of the OECD and the European Union*: The Republic of Cyprus is recognised by all members of the United Nations with the exception of Turkey. The information in this report relates to the area under the effective control of the Government of the Republic of Cyprus.

Source: EU-SILC 2013.

Problems with geographical access are also reported

Latvia also has some problems with geographical access to care, particularly in rural areas. Some challenges in rural areas are to be expected, given the falling population, migration of younger generation to urban areas in Latvia and out of Latvia, and reports of GPs leaving rural areas, or reaching retirement without being replaced (see Chapter 1). There appears to be a tendency for rural GPs to have much higher patient lists; Mitenbergs et al., 2012 report that almost 15% of GPs, mostly located in rural areas, have 2000 patients and more, while about 10% of GPs have only 1 000 patients or less (mostly in urban areas).

Geographical distribution of secondary and tertiary services through the country can also pose a problem, with many services concentrated in urban areas (particularly in or around Riga). The introduction of free hotel-type accommodation for low income groups when they travel for treatment (typically for day-surgery) could be expected to mitigate this problem in part (see Box 2.1).

Problems with access to social care and long-term care are also concerns. Long-term care (LTC) has only recently started to be reimbursed and remains relatively underdeveloped (see Chapter 1). Spending on LTC represents just 7% of Latvia's limited health budget. As Latvia's population ages, LTC needs can be expected to increase, exacerbated by high levels of out-migration of Latvia's working-age population, and high numbers of single-child families. Latvia is aware of this challenge, and a recently published World Bank Technical Assistance report on Active Ageing gives further in-depth analysis and recommendations on this area. There are also numerous OECD countries examples from which Latvia could learn: countries such as Japan have much extensive experience in developing LTC models (see OECD, 2013, as well as Chapter 3 of this report).

Several steps should be considered to reduce geographical and economic barriers to accessing health care

Decisions about health system coverage, benefit basket, cost sharing and application of exemptions vary significantly between OECD. Frequently, extent of cost sharing depend on health expenditure levels, and the need to raise revenue within the health system (see also Chapter 1); in Latvia, it is unlikely that cost sharing could be reduced substantially without an increase in other sources of health spending. It should also be noted that out-of-pocket spending has risen across OECD countries in recent years (OECD, 2015f). Nonetheless, there are some steps that Latvia could take to reduce dependency on out-of-pocket funding of the health system. An assessment of the feasibility, and potential impact, of expanding cost-sharing exemptions should be undertaken. Re-introducing exemptions to low-income households and to patients with chronic conditions would be two avenues for consideration.

In terms of considering ways to reduce geographical barriers to accessing care, there are several steps that Latvia could take. First, the potential problems associated geographical barriers in accessing care could be better understood if a broader range of data was systematically collected. Data on geographic distribution of physicians, including primary care physicians, would be a good starting point. An understanding of particular pressures access to primary care for rural populations is particularly needed, given Latvia's focus on moving care out of hospital and inpatient settings. The new professional registry system described in Chapter 1 could well ameliorate availability of data available for developing human resource strategies.

Second, Latvia needs a mix of measures to develop and adequately distribute human resources, to tackle the foreseen shortage of certain health professionals, and to develop existing human resource skills. Such elements could be brought together in a comprehensive workforce plan.

Finally, new and innovative ways of maximising the utility of existing health resources for rural populations could be considered. This should include maximising the contribution of all health professionals. Pharmacists, for instance, could take a greater role in managing chronic conditions, and the role of nurses and physicians' assistants could be expanded. Such possibilities are considered in Chapter 3. A particularly interesting example of adapting existing health care facilities to better meet local needs in a remote area, while maintaining focus on maximising the efficient use of resources, can be found in Fosen, Norway (see Box 2.2).

Box 2.2. Transforming local services to meet population needs through an integrated care model in Fosen, Norway

The peninsula of Fosen in central Norway is an impressive example of a sophisticated and patient-centred integrated care model, as well as an example of an approach that maximises the utility of existing resources, while adapting them to meet local population needs.

In Fosen, following nearly three decades of development, a well-established district medical centre (Fosen DMC) and a public health centre are now in place. Locating appropriate services close to need was a priority in Fosen; Fosen is a peninsula consisting of seven municipalities, with a population of about 25 500, where it takes between one and three hours by boat or car to the nearest hospital. Fosen DMC, located on the Fosen peninsula, provides services including inter-municipal health promotion, primary health care, a primary care on-call centre, an outpatient specialist clinic and a shared-care ward. Key to the success of the model is Fosen DMC's close co-operation with a large hospital on the Norwegian mainland, St. Olav's Hospital. Communication between the hospital and Fosen DMC is now well established, with shared data, videoconferencing units, an education programme, consistent standards and protocols used in the DMC and the hospital, and some shared staffing. As the Fosen service matured, an intermediate-care facility was created, where people could be admitted for a few days and cared for by community primary care doctors working closely with hospital specialists. With support from the specialist hospital, Fosen DMC is providing a comprehensive package of care and services closer to where residents live, minimising travel time, promoting patient-centred care, and avoiding costly admissions to the acute hospital.

In Fosen, transferring services from the hospital setting into the community resulted in high satisfaction among both patients and staff, and helped produce cost savings for the hospital. For example, when the hospital was persuaded to locate an audiologist at Fosen DMC, his lists were soon full, patients were satisfied, and patient transport costs for which the hospital had been previously liable were reduced. Evidence of staff satisfaction can be seen in very low absence rates of around 3%. Patient satisfaction surveys are frequently complimentary, and quality of life scores are comparable with those of the previous model of care. The shared-care model is also very cost effective. For example, more than three-quarters (78%) of patients admitted to local observation beds in Fosen were classified NACA class 3 – that is, patients who otherwise would normally be admitted to specialist services. This reflects the significant contribution that the DMC has made to preventing hospitalisation. Additionally, 63% of all patients admitted to an observation bed were discharged home after a maximum 36 hours, equivalent to savings of 230 bed days per year. Very few of those sent home were subsequently readmitted. The DMC has also shortened the average length of stay for patients undergoing hip or knee replacement surgery by providing an alternative site for hospitalisation, as well as an enhanced rehabilitation service focused on getting people home as soon as they are well enough to do so.

Box 2.2. Transforming local services to meet population needs through an integrated care model in Fosen, Norway

Additionally, the establishment of the Fosen DMC and broad range of co-located services did not depend on the building of new facilities. Large investments in new buildings were unnecessary, with emphasis instead turning to a smart use of existing infrastructure. An under-occupied nursing home was converted to be used as part of the DMC facilities, for instance. An analysis of the region's demographics prompted a replacement of one of the region's maternity units with intermediate beds for acute admissions, post-discharge recuperation and specialist rehabilitation, to better reflect the needs of the local population and increasing elderly population.

The annual "quota" system for organising and reimbursing health care exacerbates problems with access, coverage and out-of-pocket spending

The organisation of health services based on an annual quota system is an additional significant problem for access. Service providers are given annual limits for the services that they can provide covered by the NHS, and when these limits are reached, patients must either wait for the following year and the renewal of the quota, or pay for the services out of pocket (or with private coverage). The result of this system is that in the final months of the year it is very difficult to access certain services, and that backlogs cannot be cleared until the new year.

Health care institutions are expected to plan for the appropriate use of health care services and provision across the year, and distribute them equally month-by-month. Each month the National Health Service gathers information on waiting times at medical institutions and publishes monthly figures on the NHS website homepage. This information can be used by patients in planning their care. Access has been reported to worsen towards the end of the year. The impact of service quotas, however, could still be expected to be seen on waiting times for services through the year

Some evidence of quite significant waiting times in Latvia is available. For hip fracture surgery initiation after admission to the hospital only 50% of patients in Latvia have surgery within two days, compared to above 80% in most reporting OECD countries (see Figure 2.2). For cancer care while average time for referral from GP to specialist is relatively fast – ten days on average – time from diagnosis to start of treatment is much longer, typically 30 days across all cancers (see Table 2.1; OECD, 2013c). However, these data have not been broken down across the year, meaning that the impact of quotas increasing waiting times at the end of the year is not easily assessed. Additionally, some of the ways in which service coverage in the Latvian health system is organised appear to hinder quality of care. In particular, a "negative list" for reimbursement excludes certain services and goods from NHS coverage. For instance, thrombolysis for ischemic stroke is excluded, despite this running contrary to evidence on international best practice. In such cases hospitals would be left to cover the cost of medication from elsewhere in their budget. Some other procedures that might be expected to be systematically included, for example thoracic surgery and some neurological procedures, are also not included. In such examples there appears to be a gap between established national clinical guidelines, and the NHS tariff. While the need to control spending is clearly key in the Latvian health system, without making recommended services and goods systematically available, access to appropriate services and quality of care will continue to suffer.

Figure 2.2. Hip fracture surgery after admission to the hospital, 2013 (or nearest year)

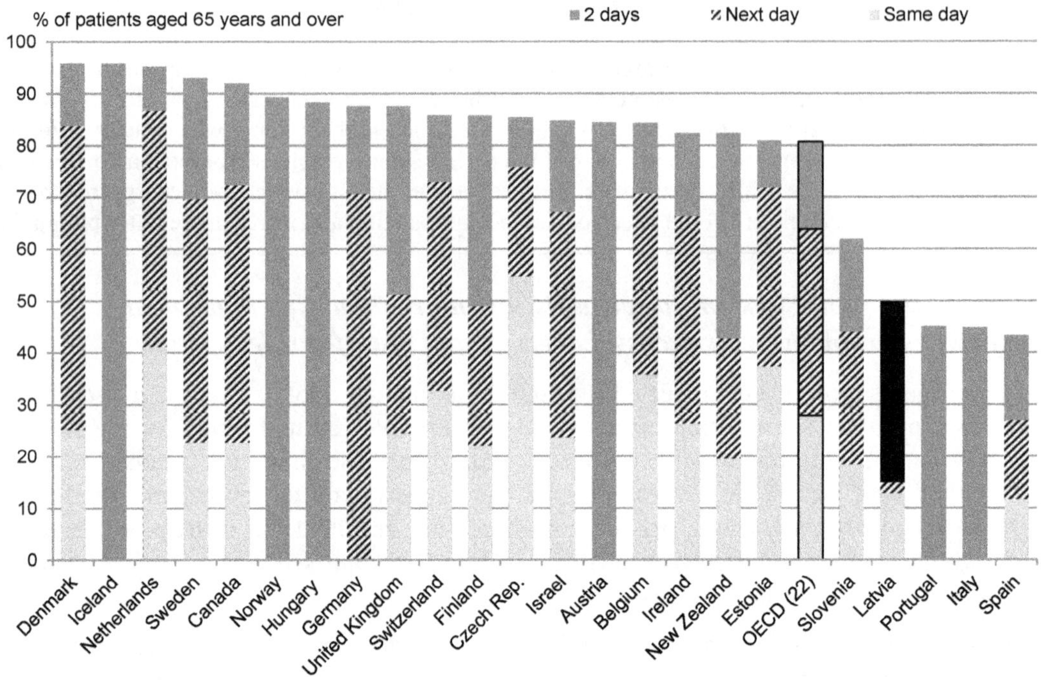

Note: Three-year average for Iceland.

Source: OECD Health Statistics 2015, http://dx.doi.org/10.1787/health-data-en.

To some degree, waiting times could be accepted as a way of managing demand for care, balancing demand with available resources. Latvia does have some mechanisms in place which prioritise services for those with the greatest need, for example children and pregnant women (Mitenbergs et al., 2012The fact that the quotas for services are exhausted by the end of the year may suggest that quota levels are insufficient, and that investment is needed to raise the threshold. Carefully assessing the relationship between demand, waiting lists, and the rate at which quotas of services are consumed is a first step. While the answer may well, in part, be increased investment in service availability, lessons from other countries where increased investments have not on their own solved the waiting times problem (see Box 2.3), should be kept in mind.

Table 2.1. Average waiting time between cancer diagnosis and initial treatment (surgery, radiotherapy and/or chemotherapy), 2010

	Breast cancer	Cervical cancer	Colorectal cancer	Lung cancer	All cancers
Canada	30 days (median	20 days (median)	21 days (median)	29 days (median)	25 days (median)
Cyprus[1, 2]	17 days	11 days	8 days	10 days	11 days
Czech Republic*	Weeks not months	Weeks not months	Weeks not months	Weeks not months	Weeks not months
France	21 days	-	-	38 days	-
Hungary*	14-21 days	14-21 days	14-21 days	14-21 days	14-21 days
Iceland*	≤ 7 days	≤ 7 days	≤ 7 days	≤ 7 days	≤ 7 days
Israel*	Radiotherapy: 15-45 days	Radiotherapy: 15-45 days	Radiotherapy: 15-45 days	Radiotherapy: 15-45 days	Radiotherapy: 15-45 days
Japan*	Same day-weeks	Same day-weeks	Same day-weeks	Same day-weeks	Same day-weeks
Latvia	30 days (median)	30 days	30 days	30 days	30 days
Luxembourg*	≤ 3 days	≤ 3 days	≤ 3 days	≤ 3 days	≤ 3 days
Malta*	Weeks not months	Weeks not months	Weeks not months	Weeks not months	Weeks not months
Netherlands	25 days	15 days	10-50 days (up to 1st treatment for rectum and colon cancers)	21 days	Approx. 40 days
Norway*	2-4 weeks	-	-	-	-
Poland*	3-12 weeks	3-6 weeks	4-8 weeks	4-6 weeks	4-6 weeks
Scotland	24 days	-	23 days	25 days	-
Slovak Republic*	7-21 days	7-21 days	7-21 days	7-21 days	7-21 days
Slovenia*	≤ 1 month	≤ 1 month	≤ 1 month	≤ 1 month	-
Sweden	19 days	Weeks not months	Weeks not months	Weeks not months	Weeks not months
Turkey*	Weeks not months	Weeks not months	Weeks not months	Weeks not months	Weeks not months

Note: Data for the Netherlands, Scotland and Sweden refer to 2008 and for Canada, Israel, Korea, Latvia and Poland to 2009. For Germany, data for cervical cancer refer to 2010 while data for other cancers refer to 2009. For French data, waiting time for breast cancer refers to 2007 while that for lung cancer refer to 2003. Countries with * refer to those in which experts provided estimated waiting times. Cancer diagnosis refers to the first day of cancer diagnosis in Korea.

1. *Note by Turkey:* The information in this report with reference to "Cyprus" relates to the southern part of the Island. There is no single authority representing both Turkish and Greek Cypriot people on the Island. Turkey recognises the Turkish Republic of Northern Cyprus (TRNC). Until a lasting and equitable solution is found within the context of the United Nations, Turkey shall preserve its position concerning the "Cyprus issue".

2. *Note by all the European Union Member States of the OECD and the European Union*: The Republic of Cyprus is recognised by all members of the United Nations with the exception of Turkey. The information in this report relates to the area under the effective control of the Government of the Republic of Cyprus.

Source: OECD HCQI Questionnaire on Systems of Cancer Care; OECD (2013), *Cancer Care: Assuring Quality to Improve Survival,* OECD Health Policy Studies, OECD Publishing, Paris, http://dx.doi.org/10.1787/9789264181052-en.

Box 2.3. Policies to address waiting times in OECD countries

OECD work on waiting times for elective surgery across thirteen countries holds some lessons for Latvia. When reflecting on the policy implications for Latvia from these countries' experiences, the fact that these lessons are drawn in large part from elective treatments should be kept in mind.

Whether a health system has waiting times, and across which procedures, depends in part on institutional characteristics and levels of health care resources. Countries with no waiting times tend to spend more on health and have higher hospital capacity. Long waiting times for elective treatments generally tend to be found in countries that combine public health insurance with zero or low patient cost sharing and constraints on capacity. Long waiting times are found less often in countries with social insurance that low choice of provider, but there are some social insurance systems with below average spending that do have waiting times for elective care.

Over the past decade, waiting time guarantees have become the most common and effective policy tool to tackle long waiting times, but are only effective if enforced. There are two approaches to enforcement: setting waiting time targets and holding health providers to account for achieving the targets, or allowing patients to choose alternate health providers, including the private sector, if patients have to wait beyond a maximum time. Variations on this approach have been taken in the United Kingdom, Finland, Portugal, the Netherlands and Denmark.

Supply-side waiting time policies such as funding or productivity increases, by themselves, are usually not successful. Generally, there is a short-term burst of funding that initially reduces waiting times, but then waiting times increase, and occasionally return to even higher levels when the temporary funding runs out.

Table 2.2. Policies to address waiting times in OECD countries

Policies		Commonly used	Potential effect on waiting times
Supply-side policies	1. Increased production in the public sector by funding extra activity	6/13 countries	Weak
	2. Contracting with private sector	6/13 countries	Weak
	3. Sending patients abroad	3/13 countries	Weak
	4. Increased productivity by introducing activity-based financing (DRGs)	3/13 countries	Medium
	5. Increased choice of providers	5/13 countries	Medium
	6. Improved management of waiting lists		Medium
Demande-side policies	1. Explicit guidelines to prioritise patients	7/13 countries	Medium
	2. Subsidise private insurance	5/13 countries	Weak
Combined policies	1. Waiting-time guarantees	13/13 countries	Weak
	2. With sanctions	3/13 countries	Strong
	3. With choice and competition	6/13 countries	Strong

The introduction of activity-based funding (DRGs) can help improve hospital productivity and, more importantly for waiting times, is often one of the key components in introducing choice and competition which can lower waiting times. In general, it appears that a combination of sufficient supply, payment systems that reward activity for both specialists and hospitals, and limited constraints on hospital spending are associated with low waiting times. However, these policies tend to be expensive.

A complementary approach to reduce waiting times is to implement demand-side policies in order to reduce or shift the demand for elective treatments. The most successful demand-side approach is to introduce tools to improve clinical prioritisation for elective treatments, though need thresholds can be difficult to establish and implement; clinical prioritisation tools have been used most widely in New Zealand with some success. In some countries, such as Norway and Australia, clinical prioritisation is linked to waiting time guarantees, with different guarantees depending on the level of need.

Source: Siciliani, L., M. Borowitz and V. Moran (eds.) (2013), *Waiting Time Policies in the Health Sector: What Works?*, OECD Health Policy Studies, OECD Publishing, Paris, http://dx.doi.org/10.1787/9789264179080-en.

Access to pharmaceuticals is limited and more funding is needed to assure adequate access

Given the mutual recognition procedures and the use of assessment undertaken abroad, there is no drug lag in Latvia and market authorisation is given without delay. But according to the NHS, out of 7 000 products authorised, only 900 are included in the positive list for reimbursement. The coverage is particularly low for newly-developed drugs. For instance, Herceptin was authorised in 2004, but was included in the positive list only in 2010, representing a relatively long time to reach coverage decisions compared with many OECD countries (OECD, 2013a). Reimbursement may also be permitted for patients who meet precisely defined criteria, leading to further difficulties in drug access. This sometimes leads to inappropriate diagnosis coding as this can be a way to assure access to certain drugs for the vulnerable patients.

Limited access to pharmaceuticals is reflected in patterns of spending. Per capita spending on pharmaceuticals is USD PPP 306 in Latvia, much lower than the OECD average of USD PPP 515 (Figure 2.3). However, the share of out-of-pocket payment for pharmaceuticals is very high, accounting for 18% of current health expenditure, compared with the OECD average of 7%. This suggests access to pharmaceuticals can be challenging in the country, particularly among low income groups. Latvia needs to assure an adequate level of access to pharmaceuticals with additional financial resources.

As done in OECD countries, Latvia tries to promote the use of generic medications. The first prescription of a NHS-reimbursed pharmaceutical product needs to include its International Non-proprietary name, pharmacists are obliged to offer the cheapest version. If a pharmacy does not have the cheapest version, it needs to cover the difference between the cheapest and the available version. For other prescriptions, pharmacists are allowed to substitute pharmaceutical products prescribed with the trade name to generics if the prescribing doctor has not forbidden this possibility Reference pricing was introduced in 2011 and this has contributed to savings of EUR 8 million. While improvements in the share of generics in terms of both value and volume were made between 2011 and 2012, the balance between generic pharmaceuticals and brand name products has been stable since then.

Latvia can do more to increase efficiency gains in this area. For example, in order to further develop generic markets, several OECD countries have introduced financial incentives for physicians, pharmacists and patients. OECD countries have also implemented price cuts achieved through negotiations with pharmaceutical manufacturers, application of compulsory rebates, and reduction of package sizes. Latvia can also consider undertaking an assessment on drug use to assure safe and cost-effective pharmaceutical use. This can be facilitated by the step-wise introduction of e-health started in 2016.

Figure 2.3. Expenditure on pharmaceuticals per capita, 2013 (or nearest year)

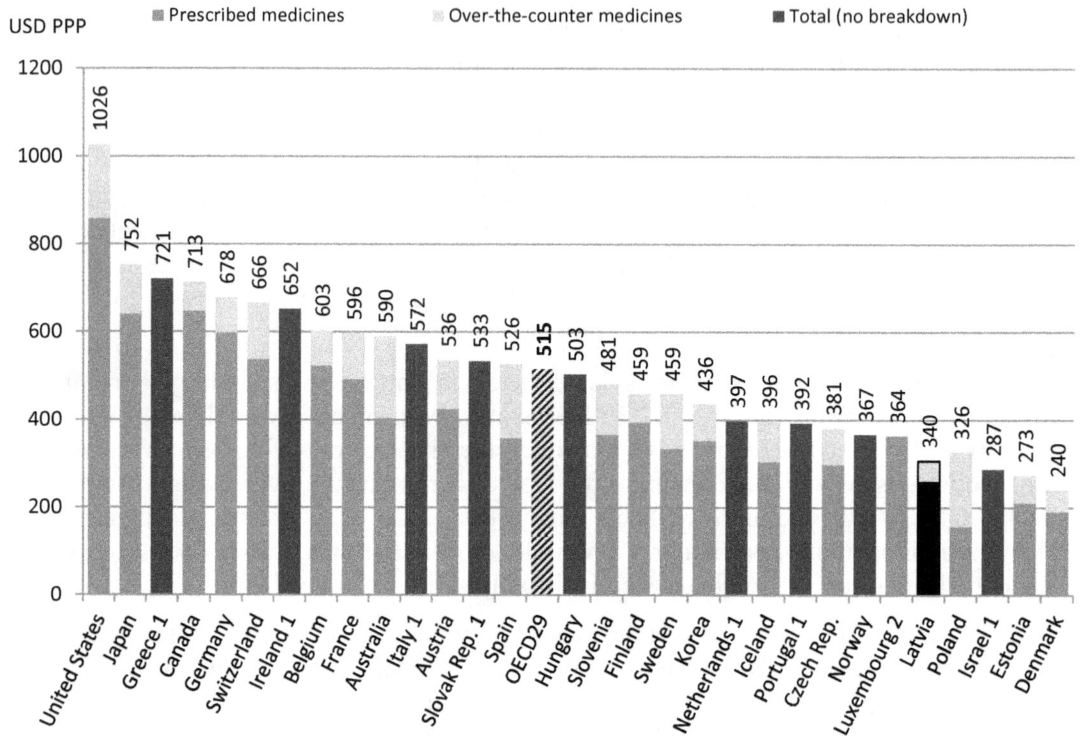

1. Includes medical non-durables (resulting in an over-estimation of around 5-10%).

2. Excludes spending on over-the-counter medicines.

Source: OECD Health Statistics, 2015, http://dx.doi.org/10.1787/health-data-en.

Figure 2.4. Generic medicines market in Latvia, 2011-14

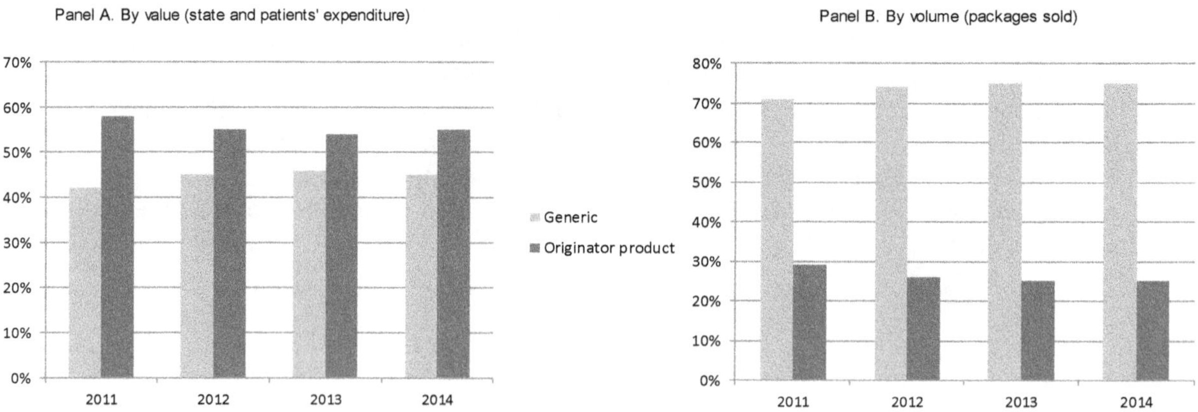

Source: Latvian State Agency of Medicines.

2.2. Quality of health care provision

Reporting on health care quality in Latvia is improving, but could be strengthened further

In 2015 Latvia was able to report on many, although not all, OECD Health Care Quality Indicators (HCQI) (Box 2.4). Latvia's ability to provide this fairly good range of HCQI data is promising, and facilitates benchmarking across against OECD countries across a series of core domains of quality.

A first step in terms of improving the availability of information on quality in Latvia will be broadening the indicators which Latvia systematically collects on quality of care. Those HCQI data that Latvia did not report in 2015, or for which data quality issues meant that publication was not possible, include the following: congestive heart failure hospital admission, major lower extremity amputation in adults with diabetes, detailed prescribing data (e.g. diabetic individuals with ≥ one prescription of cholesterol lowering medication in the last year), surgical complications, obstetric trauma, inpatient suicide amongst patients with a psychiatric disorder, and patient experience indicators.

More attention is needed to indicators of quality of care, and basic information collection around dimensions of quality such as safety. For instance, there is no national system for adverse event reporting, and no information on hospital acquired infections. Some quality indicators are available at a national level (see Box 2.4), and should be able to be broken down to a hospital level, but it is not clear that these indicators are consistently used by policy makers, managers, or health care professionals. Information on care quality at primary care level is also weak.

Box 2.4. Indicators of health care quality reported in Latvia

At the date of publication, the following indicators of health care quality were available in Latvia:

- Mortality within 30 days of hospitalisation of patients hospitalised with acute myocardial infarctions;
- Mortality within 30 days of hospitalisation of patients hospitalised with haemorrhagic or ischemic stroke;
- Emergency rehospitalisation at the same hospital within 30 days of patients with schizophrenia, schizotypal disorders or delusions;
- Traumas resulting from performed procedures (additional diagnosis) and foreign items left in the body (additional diagnosis) per 100 hospital discharges;
- Post-surgery pulmonary embolism or deep vein thrombosis (additional diagnosis) per 100 hospital discharges;
- Data on III and IV degree perineal tears during vaginal childbirth (with or without a device) in Latvia by medical treatment institution;
- Deliveries by caesarean section and cases of complications at childbirth (percentage of patients from the total number of deliveries);
- Average number of hospital days per patient and average occupancy of hospital beds;
- Proportion of hospitalisation cases by admissions departments.

Box 2.4. Indicators of health care quality reported in Latvia *(cont.)*

Once a year the NHS in co-operation with the CDPC process the data. The obtained information is published on the website of the NHS (http://www.vmnvd.gov.lv/lv/503-ligumpartneriem/operativa-budzeta-informacija/valsts-budzeta-lidzeklu-izpildes-analize-stacionaros).

Once per quarter the NHS publishes updated statistical data on its website, which includes the following:

- Overview on in-patient health care financing;
- Data on 1-2 day long hospitalisation cases;
- Proportion of hospitalised patients out of the total number of patients seen at admissions departments;
- Data on the levels of emergency care indicated by medical treatment institutions on in-patient cards;
- Proportion of childbirth/delivery services;
- Data on patients under observation in admissions departments;
- Discharged patients who have been rehospitalised on the same or next day (except patients whose next hospitalisation is for care or rehabilitation).

Going beyond the core OECD HCQI indicators, numerous OECD countries – such as Denmark, Israel, Portugal, Norway and the United Kingdom – have comprehensive data infrastructures from which Latvia could learn. These include more sophisticated ways to capture quality in primary care settings (see Chapter 3), as well as ways of measuring outcomes and patient experiences in health systems.

Latvia will also need to do more to systematically and extensively draw on health system data to inform decision making, and fully understand quality of care, which is discussed further in Section 2.5.

Based on available indicators quality of care appears mixed

Based on available indicators of quality, the Latvian primary care sector appears to be performing relatively well, while there are more significant shortcomings in the hospital sector. "Avoidable admissions" for diabetes and COPD are both below the OECD average, which could suggest that the primary care sector is providing effective management in the community. The quality of primary care is discussed in further detail in Chapter 3.

Indicators of the quality of care in hospitals, however, give much more cause for concern. For both mortality following acute myocardial infarction (AMI) and mortality following stroke, Latvia has the highest (when the patient-based indicator is taken) or second-highest (for the admission-based indicator) rate of mortality amongst all OECD countries. Mortality in the 30 days following AMI or stroke is a good indicator of quality of acute care, including the robustness of processes of care such as timely transport of patients and effective medical interventions, and the delivery of most appropriate treatment, for example thrombolytic treatment for ischemic stroke, and treatment in dedicated stroke units. Based on these indicators there appear to be some major shortcomings in the quality of acute care that is delivered in Latvia. Furthermore, mortality following AMI and stroke (patient-based indicator) appeared to worsen between 2008, although this may to some extent reflect improved data accuracy (Figures 2.5 and 2.6).

Figure 2.5. Thirty-day mortality after admission to hospital for AMI based on patient data, 2003 to 2013 (or nearest years)

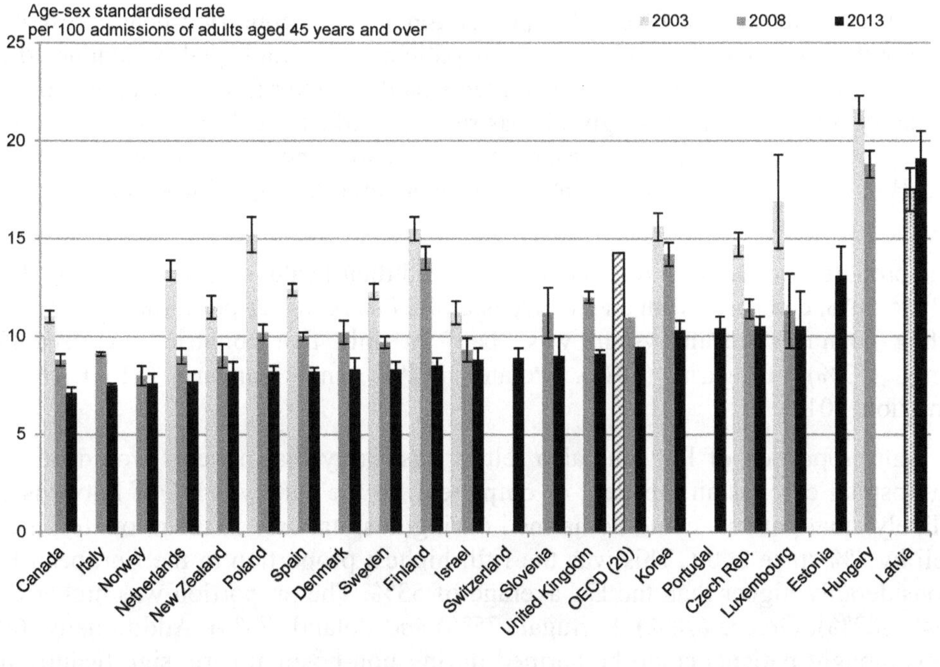

Note: 95% confidence intervals represented by H. Three-year average for Luxembourg. AMI: Acute myocardial infarction.
Source: OECD Health Statistics 2015, http://dx.doi.org/10.1787/health-data-en.

Figure 2.6. Thirty-day mortality after admission to hospital for ischemic stroke based on patient data, 2003 to 2013 (or nearest years)

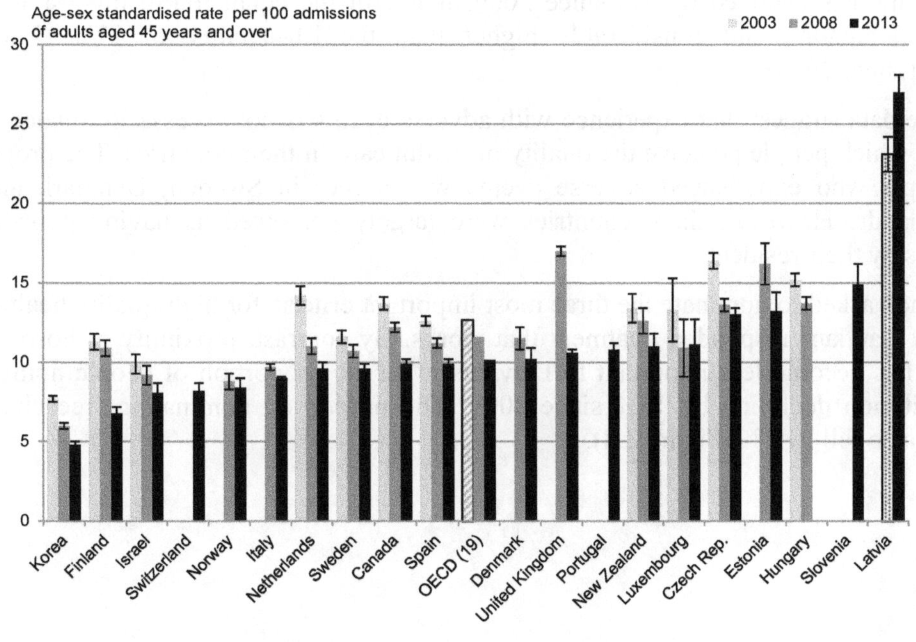

Note: 95% confidence intervals represented by H. Three-year average for Luxembourg.
Source: OECD Health Statistics 2015, http://dx.doi.org/10.1787/health-data-en.

Latvians have an unfavourable view of their health system's quality, and many report experiencing an adverse event while receiving health care

Latvians do not have a favourable perception of their country's health system. In a survey for the European Commission about patient safety and quality conducted at the end of 2013, only 47% of Latvian respondents said the overall quality of health care in their country was "good". Although this has risen by 10% since 2009, it still falls far short of the EU average of 71%. Only four countries had a poorer response rate – Poland (32%), Bulgaria (29%), Greece (26%) and Romania (25%) (European Commission, 2014).

The proportion of Latvian respondents who said their health system was "bad" declined by 12% to 50%, compared with an EU average of 27%. A higher proportion of respondents said their country's health system was "bad" in only five countries – Greece (74%), Romania (73%), Bulgaria (68%), Poland (62%) and Hungary (51%) (European Commission, 2014).

A high proportion of Latvians also felt it was likely that patients would be harmed during hospital care, as an inpatient or outpatient. In the survey, 71% of Latvians said it was "likely" that patients could be harmed during hospital care in their country, although this fell by 4% since 2009. This was the fifth highest proportion in the European Union, and considerably higher than the EU average of 53%. The proportion was higher only in Cyprus[1,2] (82%), Greece (78%), Portugal (75%) and Poland (73%). Additionally, 69% of Latvians thought patients could be harmed during non-hospital care, significantly higher than the EU average of 50% (European Commission, 2014).

Latvians were also among the most likely to have experienced adverse events when receiving health care. Of respondents who were asked if they or a family member had ever experienced an adverse event while receiving health care, 39% said yes (Figure 2.7). While this has declined by 4% since 2009, it is still the equal fourth highest with the United Kingdom, and considerably higher than the EU average of 27% (European Commission, 2014).

The data suggest that experience with adverse events is not necessarily related to the way in which people perceive the quality of health care in their countries. The proportion of people who experienced adverse events was higher in Sweden, Denmark and the Netherlands. However, these countries were largely perceived as having good health systems by their residents.

When asked to nominate the three most important criteria for high-quality health care, 51% of Latvians responded treatment that works. By contrast, proximity of hospital and doctor has become less important to Latvians, with the proportion of people nominating this criterion declining by 15% since 2009. The proportion nominating free choice of doctor also fell by 7% (Figure 2.8).

Figure 2.7. Proportion of survey respondents who say they or their family experienced an adverse event when receiving health care, 2013

Percentage of respondents

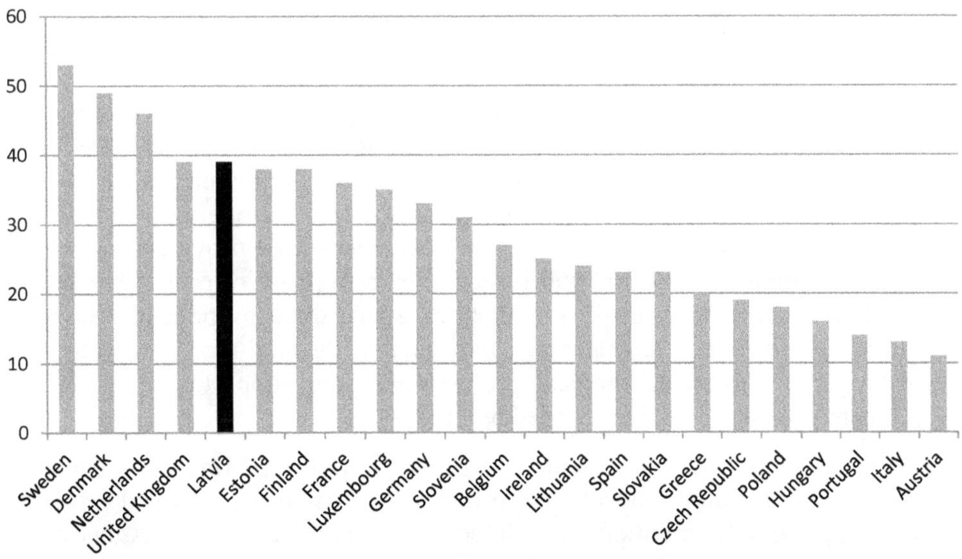

Source: Data from European Commission (2014), *Special Eurobarometer 411: Patient Safety and Quality of Care Report*.

Figure 2.8. Most important criteria for high-quality health care for Latvians, 2013[1]

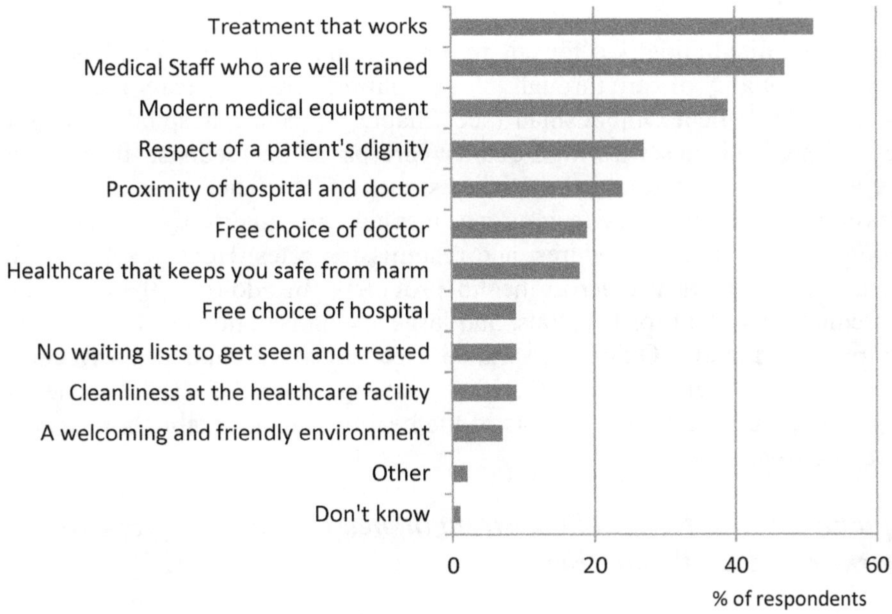

1. Respondents were asked to name up to three criteria that they associated with high-quality health care.

Source: Data from European Commission (2014), *Special Eurobarometer 411: Patient Safety and Quality of Care Report*.

Quality assurance mechanisms focus on safety but not quality of care

Quality assurance in Latvia is secured primarily through the Health Inspectorate, and the State Agency for Medicines. Some quality improvement initiatives are in place, for example hospital-specific efforts, and participation of acute hospitals in voluntary accreditation, but these efforts are more limited and ad-hoc.

The Health Inspectorate (HI) is responsible for assuring quality of care. HI evaluates NHS providers and health professionals, checking compliance with national regulations. Every year, 4 500 providers, equivalent to 10% of all health care providers, are inspected. The standards used for inspection focus on minimum requirements such as staffing numbers.,. The HI also monitors compliance against clinical guidelines. In cases where the HI assesses that NHS contracts have not been respected, providers are penalised; every year, approximately EUR 300 000 is recovered as a result of provider penalties. HI also investigates complaints related to medical care submitted by patients. Based on HI assessment patients can receive financial compensation through the treatment risk fund. HI also manages a register of medical professionals and support staff, and monitors budget and management of services funded by the NHS.

The State Agency for Medicine, under the supervision of the Ministry of Health, takes charge of assuring the safety and clinical effectiveness of pharmaceutical products and medical equipment based on national and international regulations. The Agency certifies pharmaceutical companies, gives a market authorisation of pharmaceuticals based on assessment of their safety and clinical effectiveness, and undertakes a register of authorised pharmaceuticals and medical devices. Furthermore, the Agency shares information with professionals and the public, calling for vigilance in relation to the appropriate use of, and safety issues related to, pharmaceuticals. The evaluation of medical devices is also undertaken but is not as systematic, covering only nationally-manufactured equipment.

There are some limited initiatives for quality improvement. For instance, hospitals are expected to improve quality of care through internal multidisciplinary team meetings, and collaboration with the Patient Ombudsman (see Chapter 1). Some hospitals also have a system to reward professionals with high quality care based on feedback from patients. Providers are also required to establish "quality strategies" for each year. Furthermore, several professional associations try to improve hospital care quality by monitoring and evaluating complications after procedures, and readmission rates. However, these efforts are not undertaken systematically across health providers. In addition, there is a small voluntary accreditation system for hospitals, and large specialised hospitals are starting to look to acquire accreditation. Quality assurance mechanisms around primary care are more systematic, and offer opportunities for learning from OECD countries (see Chapter 3). Quality assurance for other areas of the health system, notably home care and long-term care, are weak however.

The basic quality architecture could be strengthened and there is scope for Latvia to learn from OECD countries

Based on the indicators of quality of care in Latvia, action around care quality is needed, particularly around acute care. Attention should be turned towards strengthening quality assurance mechanisms, and encouraging quality improvement. Many of the initial building blocks of a quality assurance architecture are in place – workforce training in compliance with EU regulations, regular inspections of all providers – including GPs –

from an independent inspectorate (the HI), a requirement that providers establish "quality strategies" for each year, hospital accreditation systems, established clinical guidelines, and some clear efforts to reflect patients' views through patient satisfaction surveys and meetings with consumer and user groups (see Chapter 1). However, there is clear scope for improvement of outcomes in Latvia, and further steps to build quality assurance and drive attention to quality improvement should be taken.

There is great potential for Latvia to learn from the experiences of OECD countries' approaches to quality assurance and improvement. A closer review of clinical processes in Latvia – for example through clinical audits, and/or further use and development of performance and outcome indicators – would help narrow focus to particular areas for attention. Given Latvia's poor performance on indicators of quality of care in the acute hospital sector appropriate actions could be taken around the use of and completeness of clinical guidelines, developing rigorous standards of care for providers, and encouraging excellence through the application of a broader array of quality incentives. Chapter 3 also gives recommendations around strengthening quality assurance and improvement in the primary care sector. The availability and use of appropriate data on health care quality is also clearly central to quality assurance and quality improvement efforts. The collection, expansion, and better exploitation of health care quality and performance data is discussed below and in Section 2.5.

Use of clinical guidelines is not systematically monitored

Clinical guidelines in Latvia are developed by professional organisations of medical practitioners, medical treatment institutions and certain institutions of higher education, and submitted to the NHS for registration in the database of guidelines to be used in medical treatment. The Medical Treatment Law (Regulation No. 469) stipulates that medical treatment should be performed in line with approved clinical guidelines,. The priority that Latvia has given to developing clinical guidelines based on international best practice, and approving them for the NHS in a nationally standardised and consistent way, is encouraging. The fact that treatments required under the guidelines are not always covered or covered in their entirety by the NHS is of more concern (Mitenbergs et al., 2012).

Latvia should continue the development and publication of clinical guidelines, and also take steps to systematically monitor the extent to which clinical guidelines are – or can be – followed by providers. While commendable progress has been made on developing and approving guidelines, the number of clinical guidelines in use remains relatively limited when compared to OECD countries. While the Health Inspectorate monitors adherence to clinical guidelines as part of inspections, there is not a systematic effort to understand, nationally, regionally and locally, what percentage of care is delivered in line with clinical guidelines. If adherence to guidelines is found to be poor, either across the board or in particular areas, efforts to understand whether this is because of provider and practitioner resistance, lack of awareness, or because treatments recommended in guidelines are not covered in full by the reimbursement schedule, are needed.

There are OECD countries at the forefront of clinical guideline development and innovation from whom Latvia could learn. In Denmark, for example, the way in which clinical guidelines describe not only "what should be done", but they tend to describe "who should do what, when and where" (OECD, 2013a). Such an approach could well be a fruitful one for Latvia, and help feed into the development of more complex disease management pathways. Clinical guidelines can feed into the articulation of national evidence-based treatment pathways for diseases, as has been the case in Denmark, and in Portugal with the Integrated Care Pathway guidelines (OECD, 2015c). The *Choosing Wisely* approach, discussed in Section 2.5, would also be of considerable interest to Latvia.

A more rigorous framework for quality standards would benefit Latvia

At present, there are relatively few established minimum standards for health care provision in Latvia. The minimum standards that are used for inspections, are mostly process checks, for instance staffing numbers. Latvia is struggling to find a robust framework for quality which could be used to apply minimum standards to all providers, regardless of their size and nature. Clearly, given Latvia's relatively poor performance on a range of quality measures, establishing a comprehensive set of quality standards would be a step in the right direction.

In Australia, the introduction of a comprehensive set of national safety and quality standards has had some success, and could be a good model for Latvia to follow. The standards were sent up by the Australian Commission on Safety and Quality in Health Care (ACSQHC), to drive care of a uniformly high quality across the country. They are applied to all hospitals (private and public, across all states), covering ten priority areas (see Box 2.5). Development of the standards took over five years, and was carefully undertaken giving ample scope for broad stakeholder input. This has helped garner broad support of the standards and stakeholder buy-in. There has been broad agreement from stakeholders that the new standards are a positive move forward, promoting greater clinical involvement and more directly addressing specific quality issues than other standards. The standards are acute-care focused, and it is acknowledged that further development is required to effectively apply the standards to non-hospital care, including primary care, aged care, mental health care and community care and support. Since their development and introduction in 2013, ACSQHC has also given hospitals considerable support to help them comply with these standards. Adherence to the standards is checked as part of hospitals' accreditation process, carried out by a range of different accrediting bodies (all of which are, in turn, accredited by the ACSQHC).

Box 2.5. The implementation of national safety and quality health service standards in Australia

Australia has recently endorsed new standards of care and developed the national accreditation scheme. The nature and level of input afforded stakeholders in the development process appears to be one of the key factors for the broad acceptance of the new national standards and accreditation scheme in the health system.

The agreed standards are:

1. Governance for safety and quality in health service organisations which describes the quality framework required for health service organisations to implement safe systems.
2. Partnering with consumers which describes the systems and strategies to create a consumer-centred health system by including consumers in the development and design of quality health care.
3. Preventing and controlling health care associated infections which describes the systems and strategies to prevent infection of patients within the health care system and to manage infections effectively when they occur to minimise the consequences.
4. Medication safety which describes the systems and strategies to ensure clinicians safely prescribe, dispense and administer appropriate medicines to informed patients.
5. Patient identification and procedure matching which describes the systems and strategies to identify patients and correctly match their identity with the correct treatment.
6. Clinical handover which describes the systems and strategies for effective clinical communication whenever accountability and responsibility for a patient's care is transferred.
7. Blood and blood products which describes the systems and strategies for the safe, effective and appropriate management of blood and blood products so the patients receiving blood are safe.
8. Preventing and managing pressure injuries which describes the systems and strategies to prevent patients developing pressure injuries and best practice management when pressure injuries occur.
9. Recognising and responding to clinical deterioration in acute health care which describes the systems and processes to be implemented by health service organisations to respond effectively to patients when their clinical condition deteriorates.
10. Preventing falls and harm from falls which describes the systems and strategies to reduce the incidence of patient falls in health service organisations and best practice management when falls do occur.

The last eight standards deal with long-standing priority issues in patient safety, particularly in the hospital sector. Of particular importance is the fact that the ACSQHC has provided strong to support to health services in the implementation of the standards and the accreditation scheme. Support strategies include teleconferences with health service representatives, accreditation workbooks, implementation guides for each standard, a telephone and e-mail advice centre and mediation service for health services and accreditation agencies. Overall, the new national safety and quality standards and accreditation scheme represent important elements of the overall quality improvement architecture of the health system. There is broad agreement from stakeholders that the new standards are a positive move forward, promoting greater clinical involvement and more directly addressing specific safety issues (e.g. safe handover, identifying and responding to clinical handover) than other standards.

Source: OECD (2015), *OECD Reviews of Health Care Quality: Australia – Raising Standards*, OECD Publishing, Paris, http://dx.doi.org/10.1787/9789264233836-en.

Putting the right quality improvement incentives in place

In addition to taking further steps to *assure* that quality standards are being met, for instance through quality standards, and clinical guideline monitoring, Latvia could do more to foster quality *improvement*. Approaches that have had success in other OECD countries include the following:

- *Introducing performance metrics when contracting with hospitals.* Performance data could be used, as it is in Denmark, Portugal and Sweden, as part of annual contractual agreements. These performance criteria could be linked to specific payment mechanisms or budgets, but the most important dimension would not – initially – be the financing mechanism, but would be to make quality of care an integrated part of the local and national governance arrangements, and to use performance data more actively.

- *Broadening the use and effectiveness of performance-based payment and other financial incentives.* Latvia is at the early stages of introducing a pay-for-performance scheme to primary care, based on the UK's Quality and Outcomes Framework, which should be carefully monitored to ensure that incentives and expectations are well balanced (see also Chapter 3). In Portugal pay-for-performance has also been introduced to primary care, embedded in broader reform efforts, and may be an instructive example for Latvia (OECD, 2015; see Chapter 3). There may be scope to introduce such performance incentives more widely, but more could be done using Latvia's existing financing mechanisms. Latvia could learn from Japan, where fee schedule items and reimbursement rates are adjusted to encourage or discourage particular provider behaviours, e.g. introduction of a fee schedule item for establishing a Care Plan (OECD, 2015b).

- *Strengthening the voluntary accreditation system hospitals and expanding to other providers.* A number of OECD countries have a comprehensive accreditation programme as it exists in the United States, England, Australia, Denmark, France or Portugal. These countries are relying on increasingly sophisticated forms of accreditation to reassure payers and service users. Where a voluntary approach is taken, the objective is to encourage and recognise excellence, rather than just approve adherence to minimum standards. Latvia already has a small voluntary accreditation system in the acute hospital sector, and there is scope to strengthen this programme, as well as to extend it to other areas of care. In Portugal, the National Model of Accreditation is a voluntary programme applied to health care services, training programmes, and technical services such as imaging and laboratories. Additionally, ACSA International (an agreement between the Directorate-General of Health of Portugal and the Agency of Sanitary Quality of Andalusia) is a voluntary model that focuses on the accreditation of clinical management in clinical services, i.e. of hospital services or hospital departments, functional units of primary health care, of units of the national network of long-term care, of day hospitals or specialised hospitals. To be accredited the unit must demonstrate respect for patient rights, effective care which respects clinical guidelines, have a rational organisation of patient information and health records, and a rational usage of pharmaceuticals and technologies, demonstrate good professional competency, and have good support services. Importantly, the unit must also demonstrate engagement and consistency with set objectives and contractual obligations, and have an internal strategy for following this, as well as have a system of evaluation for collected performance indicators (which must also be communicated internally and publically).

- *Reflecting on clinical processes through clinical audits.* Clinical audits, focused on priority areas of care delivery, are one way that the quality, efficiency and outcomes of treatment pathways can be considered. For instance, a clinical audit for lung cancer care would compare practices and outcomes across providers, reflecting on variations in practice and outcomes. Findings from audits can then be shared as opportunities for learning, and feed into development of quality strategies and clinical standards. Clinical audits are more commonly seen in countries with long-established quality assurance and improvement programmes, such as Denmark, Sweden and the United Kingdom.

Latvia can learn from OECD countries to tackle the burden of cardiovascular diseases, cancer and mental health

Latvia could learn from OECD countries in providing care for cardiovascular diseases, cancer and mental health more effectively and efficiently. For all these disease groups, primary care can play a greater role particularly in prevention and diagnosis (Chapter 3).Health promotion is also important.

In terms of cardiovascular diseases,. OECD countries have managed to decrease case-fatality rates by assuring better access to high-quality acute care for patients, not only through timely transportation, but also through evidence-based medical interventions and care at high-quality specialised health facilities such as stroke units. In many countries in Europe, the "Stent 4 Life" initiative, launched in 2008, aims to improve the delivery of care and patient access to primary percutaneous coronary intervention (PCI) based on a partnership between professional associations, government representatives, industry partners and patient groups. It supports the implementation of European Society of Cardiology guidelines on the management of heart attacks, helps identify barriers to the implementation of guidelines, and defines actions to improve access to PCI in Europe. The objectives of "Stent 4 Life" include increasing the use of primary PCI to more than 70% among some patients and ensuring access 24 hours a day (OECD, 2015e).

OECD countries are using a variety of policy instruments to improve the quality of services along the entire pathway such as through the introduction of integrated care models, financial incentives for improved quality and performance, benchmarking, target setting and training. For example, France developed a monitoring framework to promote effective operation and interaction of many parts of the health system and delivery of better care over the full pathway. It includes the time of onset of symptoms to the initial management of stroke, first-line imaging, medications and assessment by a professional rehabilitation during the initial management. These indicators incorporate aspects that are part of the pre- and post-hospital phases of an acute CVD event. Furthermore, there is a strong emphasis on process-related indicators (e.g. door-to-balloon times or use of medications) that are within the realm the of health care sector control (OECD, 2015e).

In terms of cancer, survival of patients has improved for breast and colorectal cancer over the past decade at a faster pace in Latvia than many OECD countries, approaching to the OECD average. Latvia has intensified its effort to control the burden of cancer comprehensively in recent years. It has introduced national cancer control strategies in 2009 and centralised cancer care delivery by concentrating resources and expertise at specialised institutions in order to ensure high-quality care delivery and increase efficiency. It has also developed unified licensing and certification systems to train medical professionals with specialised skills in cancer care. These developments seem to have contributed to better quality of cancer care in recent years.

These promising developments can be built upon. For instance, in the Czech Republic cancer care delivery was reorganized, aiming to optimise the population coverage of comprehensive cancer centres, increasing investment at each centre. Partly due to more equal access, variations in cancer survival across regions has been reduced (OECD, 2013a; OECD, 2015b). A particular priority in Latvia concerns cervical cancer. Incidence is almost double the OECD average but the screening rate is still very low, at less than half of the OECD average. Given the HPV vaccination introduced in 2009, the incidence may likely decline in the future but more efforts need to be made to increase cervical cancer screening (Chapter 3).

With regards to mental health care, Latvia is increasingly shifting care from institutions to the community. Historically, Latvia focused on providing mental health care at institutions located in rural areas. Lessons from OECD countries for successful transition towards de-institutionalisation may be relevant. In some OECD countries, such as Italy, the United Kingdom, and the United States, the de-institutionalisation process started over 50 years ago (OECD, 2014e).

Across OECD countries, many people needing mental health care have fared well from de-institutionalisation, with patients preferring to live in more independent community settings. Appropriate care in the community must be provided, and steps must be taken to ensure that the burden of care does not fall entirely on family carers. In addition, when care is predominantly delivered away from hospitals, co-ordination becomes a bigger challenge; individuals often have a range of health and social needs that must be organised by a range of care providers, unlike the single care setting of the psychiatric hospital. To help deal with this co-ordination challenge there is scope for GPs to be involved in the ongoing care of people with severe mental illness. GPs or other primary care providers should also ensure that attention to the *physical* health of individuals with mental ill-health is provided in an appropriate manner, which can help reduce excess mortality for people with mental disorders (OECD, 2014e).

A growing number of OECD countries also allow people with a mental illness to be placed under a Community Treatment Order (CTO). These orders legally compel people experiencing severe mental ill-health to comply with treatment, without being detained in hospital. This is a less restrictive alternative to traditional in-patient involuntary treatment orders (OECD, 2014e). Nonetheless, patient rights, and appropriate representation of patient views, should be at the forefront whenever compulsory treatment orders are applied.

Investing more in primary care is also a cost-effective way of treating mild-to-moderate mental disorders like depression and anxiety. These common conditions are often highly treatable, but many people with these conditions do not receive the treatment they need. Evidence suggests that psychological treatments, especially cognitive behavioural therapy (CBT), are effective for mild-to-moderate depression and anxiety. In many OECD countries, primary care practitioners are able to refer patients to psychological therapies, although the costs of such therapies are often not reimbursed. Improving access to psychological therapies would help close the large treatment gap (OECD, 2014e).

2.3. Efficiency in the health system

Latvia has taken successful steps towards rationalising the hospital sector

In a system which is structurally under-funded, increasing efficiency in order to maximise the impact of limited resources has been, and continues to be, a major priority in Latvia. Progress in this area has been impressive in some areas; most strikingly, Latvia has closed a number of hospitals and 18 emergency departments in a reportedly effective drive to improve efficiency. Simultaneous efforts were made to move care out of the hospital sector towards community settings, to reduce admissions and length of stay in hospitals, and to prioritise outpatient care.

Latvia's push to reduce the size of the hospital sector, and move more care into the community, began in 2004 when, based on recommendations from the World Bank, the Cabinet of Ministers adopted the "Development Programme for Out-Patient and In-Patient Healthcare Service Providers" strategy. The aim of this programme was the further development of an integrated health care system through optimisation of the number and distribution of service providers, thus increasing the overall quality of provided health care services, cost efficiency and accessibility for patients. The programme and its implementation plan stipulated that as of 2005 the number of beds in-patient facilities providing state-paid services would gradually be decreased.

In 2005, Latvia had 17 218 in-patient beds(7.5 beds per 1 000 inhabitants). In 2010 there were some six thousand fewer, equivalent to 11 920 beds (5.7 beds per 1 000 inhabitants) (CDPC, 2013). The number of inpatient facilities providing state-funded services also decreased significantly, from 92 to 40, with the closure of some institutions, and the transformation of others to provide out-patient services. Financing from EU funds in the 2007-13 planning period was channelled towards improving the skills and knowledge of practitioners, transforming small hospitals into out-patient facilities and developing the infrastructure of the bigger hospitals. At the same time, there was also a decrease of nearly 15% in average duration of treatment at in-patient institutions, from an average 9.6 days in 2005, to 8.3 days in 2013 (CDPC, 2013). The number of out-patient visits, including visits to primary and secondary care specialists increased by 38% between 2005 and 2013 (taking into account Latvia's falling population), going from an average 5.2 visits per inhabitant to 7.1 visits per inhabitant (12 577 446 visits to a medical doctor in 2013, and 1 616 113 visits to doctor's assistants, midwives and nurses (CDPC, 2013).

Some examples of local innovation in driving efficiency are commendable

Some examples of local innovation in driving efficiency are also commendable, and hold lessons for OECD countries, for instance the introduction of an "observation ward" in Vidzemes Hospital in the Valmiera district, which has helped reduce hospital admissions from emergency care significantly (see Box 2.6).

Box 2.6. The development of an "Observation Ward" to reduce admissions in Vidzemes Hospital, Valmiera

In 2011 in the Vidzemes Hospital, Valmiera, the number of inpatients was 30% higher than the target number in the contract with National Health Service. Above the target, the hospital was not reimbursed for treatment provided, and so treated approximately 3 000 patients a year using the hospital's own funds. To tackle this challenge, and avoid unnecessary hospitalization several solutions were considered.

Initially, patient flows through the emergency department were reconfigured, with the intention of allocating patients directly to the appropriate ward. This rapidly reduced the number of hospitalisations, but they remained 4% higher than the target in 2012..

Other solutions were therefore considered. For instance, some patients were offered day care. However, the capacity of hospital wards where day care patients were allocated was also found to be insufficient.. Nevertheless, in the short-term the amount of inpatients did decrease slightly.

In 2014, Vidzemes hospital opened a new Observation Ward, co-financed by the European Regional Development Fund (ERDF). The new ward significantly improved patient investigation, monitoring and treatment before hospitalisation. By 2014 the total number of admitted patients was just under, for the first time, the target billable number of patients. This significant achievement is thought to be as a result of the introduction of the Observation Ward.

Source: Information provided by Vidzemes Hospital, Valmiera.

Such innovation is an encouraging sign for Latvia, and suggests that the health system leaves room for dynamic thinking, and responsiveness to local needs. Also, commendably, local hospitals appear to collaborate well with other local providers, including hospitals nearby, in seeking efficient ways of providing care at a regional level (see also Chapter 1).

There is not at present a clear way in which local best practice is shared across Latvia, and this may be worth developing. In a small country like Latvia informal connexions, and perhaps sharing of best practice in national or local publications and journals, may be sufficient. Nonetheless, regional network organisations such as those seen in Denmark and Norway may be worth considering on a smaller scale (see Box 2.7). The highly centralised Latvian health system is, clearly, very different from the highly decentralised systems in Denmark and Norway. Nonetheless, there still may be scope for some more systematic network building across the country, and more regular sharing of local experiences, successes, and challenges. The Latvian Association of Regional and Local Governments and/or the Latvian Hospitals' Association might be natural starting points for exchange of ideas. More locally comparable, provider-level data may also help stimulate dialogue about successes and challenges in different areas of the country.

Box 2.7. Facilitating sharing of local best practice in Denmark and Norway

In **Denmark** the *Danske Regioner,* or association of Danish regions, brings together all regions to develop detailed regulation following national legislating and policy setting. In Denmark national legislation increasingly sets out requirements on topics such as waiting times, safety of pharmaceuticals and adverse event reporting, and then more detailed regulation is carried out through the agreement between the national level, the regions, and the municipalities.

In **Norway** the *Kommunesektorens organisasjon,* the Norwegian Association of Local and Regional Authorities, is a national interest association for all 428 Norwegian municipalities, 19 counties, and public enterprises. KS have regular contacts with central authorities to advocate for the interest of its members, and negotiate agreements with the government. The 2012-15 agreement, for example, aimed at promoting quality initiatives in primary health care services. The agreement put great emphasis on patient participation, prevention, rehabilitation and the use of new technologies. KS actively communicates with the members, disseminates information and facilitates the exchange of experience. The regular consultations between the central government and the Norwegian Association of Local and Regional Authorities also focus on financial issues depending on the duties and responsibilities of local authorities.

Source: OECD (2013), *OECD Reviews of Health Care Quality: Denmark – Raising Standards*, OECD Publishing, Paris, http://dx.doi.org/10.1787/9789264191136-en; OECD (2014), *OECD Reviews of Health Care Quality: Norway – Raising Standards*, OECD Publishing, http://dx.doi.org/10.1787/9789264208605-en.

The Safety Net and Social Sector Reform Programme introduced after the financial crisis had a positive impact upon efficiency

The impact of the financial crisis in Latvia from 2009 led to a significant reduction in the health care budget (see Chapter 1), and a renewed need to find areas of saving, and efficiency measures. Efforts were again focused on reducing hospital services, while trying to ensure the broadest possible accessibility to services, and trying to prevent harm to population health. The following priorities were adopted: development of out-patient services (including introduction of home care, a second nurse at family doctor practices and development of day hospitals), emergency medical assistance, care for pregnant women and children, as well as preventive measures. Much of this approach was carried out as part of the Safety Net and Social Sector Reform Programme, carried out with funding assistance from the World Bank.

As well as introducing measures to protect vulnerable groups from co-payments and other barriers to access (see Section 2.1), the programme focused on the shift away from hospital care towards ambulatory and community care. Home services for chronic illnesses were targeted at keeping down hospital admissions, and free hotel-type accommodation for poorer groups facilitated day and ambulatory care. The programme also provided additional funding for primary care, through increasing GP contracts with nurses, and allowing a second nurse to be hired by GPs (see Chapter 3). An advisory telephone service connecting patients to a doctor at their GP surgery was also introduced from 2011.

In 2012 the World Bank carried out an assessment of the implementation of the Safety Net and Social Reform Programme, and found that overall the programme had a favourable impact on efficiency of health care services. Some of the measures of the programme have been integrated into Latvia's basic health budget and thereby continued, including development of out-patient health services.

Reflection on the future of the hospital sector is needed

The post-2004 wave of structural reforms in the hospital sector in Latvia is now coming to an end, but it seems clear to the Latvian Authorities that further closures and changes will need to be made. A broader – and appropriate – push to move care out of hospitals and into the community also demands reflection over the way in which hospitals are used. Additionally, the ownership of different hospital by different levels of governance, notably the ownership of municipal hospitals by municipalities, impedes more coherent planning for the whole Latvian hospital estate, and may need revisiting.

A strategic approach to further efficiency gains in the hospital sector is needed. While Latvia has already closed several hospitals and emergency departments, more hospital closures or functional changes may still be needed in order to secure high quality care that represents good value for money across the health system. Difficult decisions and compromises will need to be made, continuing to balance the priority of assuring appropriate access to services for all Latvians, and the likely need to close hospitals with lower deliver rates to promote quality and efficiency gains. A starting point would be a comprehensive mapping of services (hospital, outpatient, community and primary), including service volumes, to assess where there is slack in the system. Such an exercise would help pinpoint where services can be closed, or adapted, without a detrimental impact on access. This process could also help identify services where service volumes are too low to promote high quality care (see Box 2.8). Indeed, Latvia undertook a similar exercise prior to the reform of the emergency care system, assessing which departments were not representing good value for money, or delivering high quality.

Box 2.8. Evidence on the relationship between volume and quality in hospital services

There is an extensive academic literature on the relationship between volume and quality in hospital services. Under pressure to drive improvements in quality and reduce costs, OECD countries have often encouraged the concentration of hospital services among fewer and larger hospitals. This has provided scope for studies in this area to explore whether higher hospital volumes truly deliver improvements in quality and patients' outcomes.

Systematic reviews confirm that volumes do make a difference

Studies have shown that patients who receive care from physicians who undertake a type of surgery frequently are less likely to die or have complications. A study of some 135 studies undertaken since 1985 by Halm, Lee and Chassin (2002) found that 70% of studies demonstrated in broad terms that patients have lower mortality rates if a hospital or physician does large numbers of procedures. This finding was strongest in AIDS treatment, surgery on pancreatic cancer, oesophageal cancer, abdominal aortic aneurysms and paediatric heart problems. Weaker relationships were identified for heart surgery, surgery for other cancers and orthopaedic procedures. Consistent with these conclusions, a major study that drew on US Medicare data found that admission to hospitals with high volumes was associated with a reduction in AMI, heart failure and pneumonia (Ross et al., 2010).

A surgeon's volumes is often more important than the hospital's

Results from the systematic review suggest that surgeon volume was a more important determinant than hospital volume in the case of CABG, carotid endarterectomy, surgery for ruptured abdominal aneurysm and surgery for colorectal cancer. Another study found considerably lower mortality rates for selected cardiovascular operations and cancer resections amongst high volume surgeons than those with less experience (Birkmeyer and Nallamothu, 2007).

Box 2.8. Evidence on the relationship between volume and quality in hospital services *(cont.)*

Considering causality in the relationship between quality and volume, the surgeon and the hospital

The positive relationship between quality and volume observed in many studies also raises a question about the direction of the causality. Most studies do not monitor changes in volumes over time. The few studies which were able to draw on longitudinal data found that changes in volumes at a hospital over time had little effect on outcomes. This has important policy implications, as it suggests that there is likely to be a complex interaction between the volumes a particular surgeon does and the hospitals where high volume surgeons work in (Halm et al., 2002). Good outcomes may be associated with certain processes of care, such as routine treatment algorithms, reminders for staff and established systems of clinical flows within hospitals. To the extent that there is an observed association of lower surgical mortality at high volume hospitals, this may not necessarily reflect more skilled surgeons and fewer technical errors, but a range of other aspects of care such as patient selection of anaesthesia and post-operative care.

Source: Adapted from OECD (2013), *OECD Reviews of Health Care Quality: Denmark 2013: Raising Standards*, OECD Publishingn Paris, http://dx.doi.org/10.1787/9789264191136-en, using the following sources: Ross, J.S. et al. (2010), "Hospital Volume and 30-Day Mortality for Three Common Medical Conditions", *New England Journal of Medicine*, Vol. 362, pp. 1110-1118; Birkmeyer, J.D. and B. Nallamothu (2007), "Surgeon Volume", The Leapfrog Group, Factsheet; Birkmeyer, J.D. and C. Phibbs (2012), "Evidence-based Hospital Referral", *The Leapfrog Group*, Factsheet; Halm, E.A., C. Lee and M. Chassin (2002), "Is Volume Related to Outcome in Health Care? A Systematic Review and Methodoligic Critique of the Literature", *American College of Physicians-American Society of Internal Medicine*, Vol. 137, No. 6; Ferguson, B., T. Sheldon and J. Posnett (1997), *Concentration and Choice in Health Care*, Royal Society of Medicine Press; London.

The second step would be to establish a strategic plan focused on health system transformation and efficiency gains, with a horizon of at least five to ten years. This which should also seek to give some clarity over which services should expect to undergo restructuring or closure, and the support that will be put in place for employees and local populations during and following this process. There will be tough decisions to make around reducing the range of services offered at some hospitals, but Latvia has done this before with some success. Other countries continue to do this, for instance Denmark (OECD, 2013a).

As additional part of this two-step scoping and strategy development process, reflection on the ownership of Latvian hospitals is needed. At present, municipal hospitals are owned by municipal governments. While it is apparent that some municipal governments, and local populations, may be very invested in their local hospital, there is an argument to be made for transferring ownership (or functional governance) of all hospital to the central level. Such a move would allow for a more integrated, national system for ownership and management of the hospital estate, would allow a more strategic view and planning to be undertaken, and could also give hospitals more freedom to develop more enterprising approaches to quality and efficieny. In a resource-stretched country, central leadership could also help to rationalise the use and purchase of such high-cost medical technologies, balancing need and usage, with resource constraints and efficiency. With ownership, competencies and accountability all in one place, the central government could take a stronger role in deciding the role, function and capacity of each hospital in the country in the context of national health vision. Such a move would also allow for better planning and networking between service sectors.

Latvia should look for further ways to eliminate waste from the system

All health systems have, to varying extents, degrees of "waste", which can be targeted to reduce lost resources, improve value-for-money, and promote high quality care. By taking steps like closing low-volume or underperforming hospital departments, Latvia has been tackling waste in two ways. First, the significant resources of maintaining an underused hospital or department are being better directed elsewhere in the system, where are greater number of service users can benefit. Second, risks that with low volumes lead to poorer quality care and outcomes, which are also financially costly, are being addressed (see discussion on the relationship between volume, quality, and the rationalisation of the hospital sector, Section 2.5).

Shortcomings in the Latvian data system may mean that comprehensive analysis of potential areas of waste within the system is difficult. However, common areas of waste identified across OECD countries will be useful for Latvia to consider in seeking improve efficiency in the system. In addition to wasteful clinical care, related to variations in care and appropriate use of pharmaceuticals and medical devices, the failure to deliver care in the right settings, and effectively co-ordinated care can generate significant wasted resources. These are issues considered in Chapter 3. These also stand as both avenues to which Latvia should direct attention and the capacity of existing data systems, and as further incentives to strengthen and better exploit the health data infrastructure:

- *Variations in care and outcomes – focusing on eliminating wasteful clinical care.* While medical treatment should be based on clinical evidence, need and patient preferences, there is strong evidence that care provision is not always driven by these factors. Geographical variations in care can be significant, even when robust national clinical guidelines exist. OECD (2014c) found, for example, significant variation in inter- and intra-country procedure rates for knee and hip replacement, and caesareans. Significant variations – in procedures, treatment, and outcomes – suggest some degree of over- or under-provision of care, which raises some concerns. The *Choosing Wisely* campaign, now underway in many OECD countries, focuses on services for which there is strong evidence of over-use and associated harm and/or costs. This physician-led initiative, which started in the United States, distils complex clinical guidelines into "nuggets of evidence-based don't do's". These are intended to be shared and discussed with patients, avoiding alarm about rationing. *Choosing Wisely* is potentially a very promising avenue to reduce waste at the bed side.
- *Effective use of resources – pharmaceuticals and medical devices.* Health technologies, including pharmaceuticals and medical devices, can account for a significant part of health system expenditure. To reduce waste in this area efforts should start before resources reach the health system, with reflection on procurement processes and payment systems. In Portugal, a rationalised national approach to purchasing medical devices such as cardiac defibrillators, joint prostheses or diagnostic kits was introduced following the financial crisis (OECD, 2015c). Latvia should also be promoting the use of pharmaceutical generics – and encourage, or require pharmacies to stock and promote generic alternatives. The effective distribution of health care resources, for example testing and laboratory equipment should also be considered; it may be that expensive health technologies can be shared between providers. Use of medical resources, such as tests and diagnostic procedures, should also be considered, to eliminate unnecessary costly procedures; this is an area picked up on by the *Choosing Wisely* initiative.

As the principal purchaser the NHS could play a larger role in increasing health system efficiency through more strategic contracting

As a purchaser of health services, the NHS could also play a larger role in increasing health system efficiency by undertaking selective purchasing systematically. Already given the current availability of health information, NHS could strengthen monitoring and evaluation of provider activities and make contractual agreements only with well-performing providers to drive quality improvement. In the same vein, the NHS could look to contract more often with independent providers, on clear cost/quality criteria, with expected outcomes specified in contracts. Selective purchasing could be applied also by the private voluntary health insurance schemes by focusing not only the cost but also the quality aspects of health care. Alongside these efforts, public reporting of provider assessment should be also developed as such information could be used to promote the public in making active choice over provider for their own care.

In Portugal, significant efficiency gains have been in the hospital sector, where a comprehensive approach to improving efficiency and quality was taken. The Portuguese example, with regards to the hospital sector, is presented as a good example for Latvia to follow (Box 2.9).

Box 2.9. Strategic approaches to contracting to promote efficiency and quality in the Portuguese hospital sector

Reforms to the hospital sector in Portugal over the last decade have focused squarely on gaining efficiency and improving quality. From 2002 new forms of management have been introduced to the hospital sector to bring together quality and efficiency gains. This reform has included transforming some NHS hospitals into hospital enterprises, accompanied by the introduction of a new payment system for hospitals based on explicit contracting programme (the so-called *Contratos Programa*), and combined with an adapted DRG payment system. Under these contracts 5% of a hospital's income is linked to its quality and performance. Each year, hospitals have to commit to certain levels of activities in return for an overall yearly budget. Beyond an expected production level, the contract sets qualitative targets and quality standards.

The second policy change was the creation of public-private partnerships (PPPs) in the hospital sector. PPP hospitals are public institutions with administrative, financial and asset management autonomy under contracted private management. In this case, hospital services are jointly provided by public and private parties sharing financial, technical and operational risk. The overarching objective of creating PPP hospitals was to improve general performance in the health sector and also ensure that private funds will finance a new set of urgent hospital investments.

Source: OECD (2015), *OECD Reviews of Health Care Quality: Portugal 2015: Raising Standards*, OECD Publishing, Paris, http://dx.doi.org/10.1787/9789264225985-en.

2.4. Health system sustainability

Financial sustainability will be an ongoing challenge in coming years

As Latvia looks to strengthen the health system and drive improvements in the system, the level of resources in the system will undoubtedly be a major challenge. With just 5.3% of GDP spent on health (2013), compared to the OECD average of 8.9%, and with per capita expenditure at EUR PPP 934, Latvia spends less on health than any other OECD country. To push towards performance and care quality on a par with most OECD countries more investment is likely needed. Low and unstable levels of financing will undermine continued consistent improvements, and reliance on EU funding for some core areas – notably prevention and health promotion – is a really challenge to sustainable growth, and impedes the development of a clear ten to twenty year vision for the health system. However, for the coming period up to 2020 there are considerable financial resources allocated from the EU funds and the state budget for health promotion and prevention activities in line with the Public Health Strategy for 2014-20. Activities initiated during this EU funding period for 2014-20 will be continued into the planning period following year 2020. The Ministry of Health will also participate in the "active ageing" strategy drafting process led by the Ministry of Welfare.

Without further investments, further health system strengthening will be extremely challenging

The progress that Latvia has made in the last 20 years in consolidating health care coverage for the population, and building a robust and functional health system, is commendable. There is scope to improve efficiency and value-for-money in the Latvian health system, as Latvia has already begun to do, but there are limits to the efficiency gains that can be made without additional investment.

This review identifies a series of areas where improvements stand to be made – to improve outcomes and quality of care, system planning, access, sustainability across domains such as the data infrastructure and human resource development. Significant progress across any or all of these areas will be extremely difficult with the current level of resources in the system. While some improvements may bring efficiency gains, most will involve at least certain level of upfront investment.

To start seeing health outcomes closer to the OECD average, and make real inroads into problems with access and quality, Latvia will most likely need to increase health spending per capita to a level closer to the OECD average, and almost certainly to increase percentage of GDP spent on health closer to the OECD average. If Latvia is to make the health system strengthening a priority, a targeted, incremental increase in spending is needed, rather than a sudden cash injection, which would bring significant risks and likely limited return over time. When Latvia finds itself in a position to increase health system spending, support from the OECD and other international partners, should be sought to maximise the positive impact of additional health system investments.

Coping with changing demographics, and the ageing population, will be a challenge to sustainability

Latvia's shrinking population and low birth rate (Chapter 1), and ageing population, will present health system sustainability challenges in the years to come. First, health needs can be expected to increase. The health needs of Latvia's older population could already be judged to be high relative to OECD countries. Life expectancy at 65 was far lower in Latvia than in OECD countries, at 19 years for women and 14 years for men, compared to 21 and 18 years on average across OECD countries in 2013 (Figure 2.9). Recent Eurostat data find that *healthy* life expectancy at age 65 was 4.6 years for women (representing only 24% of their 19 remaining years of life) and 4 years for men (representing 29% of their 13.8 remaining years of life) in Latvia in 2014. This is much lower than in the EU as a whole: 8.6 years for both women and men (representing 40% of the 21.6 remaining years of life for women and 47% of the 18.2 years of life for men.) With an ageing population countries can expect multiple additional challenges, for example a higher burden of chronic disease – including multiple morbidities –, additional LTC needs, changing needs in terms of access to care, and increased risk around discharging frail elderly patients from hospital. Many of these challenges are discussed in greater detail in Chapter 3.

Second, a shrinking working-age population may put additional strain on sources of health system revenue, and put health budgets under strain given fiscal pressures generated by other age-related expenditures. With an increased old-age dependency ratio, fiscal pressures beyond the health system can be expected to include increased long-term care and social care needs, and pressure on the pension sector (World Bank, forthcoming). Furthermore, demographic challenges could create challenges for growth, and risk driving a decline in income, if steps are not taken to mitigate the impact of ageing on the economy. The World Bank sets out a series of recommendations, which include focusing on participation of older workers and women, improving productivity, and ultimately increasing fertility and/or reducing migration. These recommendations, amongst others, should feed into Latvia's "active ageing" strategy, due in 2016. When preparing this strategy the synergies between the health sector – both in terms of changing, need, budget, as well as workforce and access impacts – and other sectors, including employment and pensions, social policy, and gender, should be given due consideration.

Figure 2.9. Life expectancy at age 65 by sex, 2013 (or nearest year)

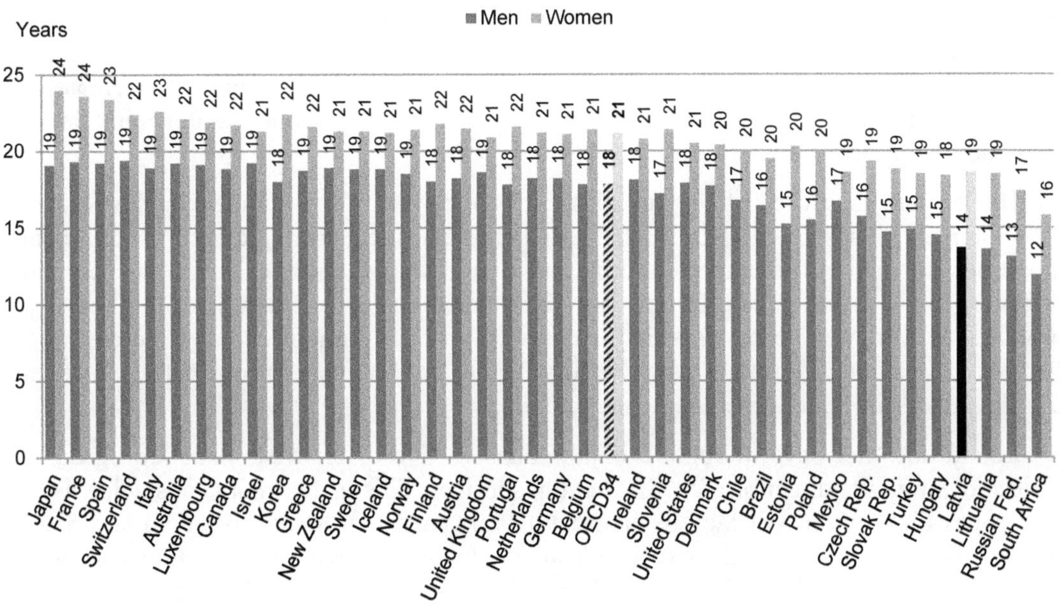

Note: Countries are ranked in descending order of life expectancy for the whole population.

Source: OECD Health Statistics 2015, http://dx.doi.org/10.1787/health-data-en.

Policy making for the health sector is hindered by high levels of instability

As already noted, Latvia has managed to make some impressive health status and health system gains in recent years, despite challenging economic circumstances. Nonetheless, sustainable policy making is a real challenge in Latvia, at all levels of the health system.

At a government level, unstable financing, a high turnover of ministers, and the under-exploitation of data on health system performance mean that policies are too often scatter-gun, and short term. To finance the health system Latvia relies not just on a high out-of-pocket contribution from patients, but also on European Union contributions (see below). This means that policy makers are particularly unsure of the budget that they will have to work with in the years to come, and it is difficult for payers and providers in the system to develop longer term strategies. To some extent, the significant financial challenges that Latvia has faced in recent years has accelerated the pace of system change and had a positive impact, for instance speeding up reforms to the hospital sectors. In other respects though, financial pressures have meant that focus is dragged back to the short term; as in most OECD countries, long-term investments in population health, for example prevention and public health, have suffered.

It is telling that Latvia does not, at present, have a strategic plan for the development of the health service, unlike most OECD countries. The National Development Plan of Latvia for 2014-20 does include some focus on health – the priority "Human Security" includes a strategic objective "Healthy and Fit for Work", which covers issues of accessibility and quality of health care services, healthy and active life style and the promotion thereof – but planning here remains in relatively general terms. Priorities for health care policy, in line with the National Development Plan, were set by the Cabinet of Ministers, but again remain fairly broad even though they seem entirely in line with shortcomings identified in this review, for instance, "to secure increased financing from the state budget for the creation of a sustainable health care system"; "to create and introduce a health care quality assurance system"; and "to continue the development and introduction of the e-health system".

Health care measures of the social security net were also included in the Strategic Development Plan of Latvia for 2010-13, which proposed a strategic goal, priorities and directions of action pertaining to the existing social-economic situation, including priorities such as consolidation of in-patient health care; efficiency of primary care provider network and team; ensuring accessibility of out-patient care by increasing the portion of financing allocated from the total health care budget for out-patient care; and ensuring accessibility of emergency medical aid.

Latvia does not have, though, a comprehensive five or ten year plan setting out the expected strategic direction for the health service. This is a major obstacle, as the challenges that Latvia will face in the next 10-20 years – an ageing population, notably, rise in chronic disease, likely rise in obesity – demand reflection, planning and action now. The Ministry of Health has elaborated the Public Health Strategy for 2014-20 (Ministry of Finance of the Republic of Latvia, 2014) setting four top priorities in public health, namely cardiovascular diseases, cancer, perinatal and neonatal health and mental health. Longer-term strategic policy planning is also needed to inform financial planning; investment in system change, innovative models of care, capital investment, and research is needed in a more sustainable way than the current one-year budgets. When reflecting on future priorities, and changing health care needs, Latvia's relatively under-developed, under-funded approach to prevention should raise particular concerns. However, under the Public Health Strategy for 2014-20 considerable financial resources from the EU funds and state budget are allocated for health promotion and prevention. Furthermore, activities initiated during this EU funding period for 2014-20 will be continued as well during the next planning period after the year 2020.

The instability at the level of national governance is carried down to regional and local levels. For example, the closure of a number of hospitals for efficiency and quality gains are seen as successful, and it is widely agreed that more hospitals should be closed or re-purposed. However, a lack of strategic planning around such closures means that hospitals, for instance, are left unsure about their viability, status, and what is expected of them.

The health system information infrastructure is relatively rich, but could be exploited further to understand system performance and efficiency

Latvia has been strengthening its health information infrastructure in recent years and has high quality health system data, allowing it to be benchmarked alongside OECD countries. With the introduction of e-health system in 2015, the availability and use of health information will be increased even more as the system will record health services delivered, tests and their results, their costs and prescription information for each patient using unique patient identifier. The provider coverage is initially limited but the system is envisaged to cover all providers in coming years. While the availability of indicators of health care quality indicators, for instance OECD HCQI, could still be expanded, Latvia is nonetheless reporting a fairly good selection of indicators (see Section 2.2).

That said, Latvia has not exploited the possibilities of utilising health information to the fullest for evidence-based policy making and quality improvement. More needs to be done to develop data-driven health planning and governance in Latvia. For example, Latvia conducts only a few health-related surveys, while many OECD countries use surveys as important tools to collect a wide range of information including on patient experience, care co-ordination and patient safety. Provider-level data, discussed in the following section, is another priority.

The NHS could undertake more systematic monitoring and assessment of health provider performance and health care utilisation by using information collected through e-health. This could be done as part of promoting better quality of care and adequate use of health care resources as done in some OECD countries such as Denmark and Portugal (see Section 2.3), as well as part of reducing waste in the system (see Section 2.5). For example, Latvia could monitor and evaluate the appropriate and inappropriate use of health care resources, services and tests results and also to ensure medication safety by monitoring prescription given by multiple professionals. In general, while privacy and data security issues are important to keep in mind, there is much that Latvia can learn from other countries in striking a balance between promoting the secondary use of data through further data linkage efforts, and protecting individual privacy.

Crucially, for a regular monitoring and evaluation, an assessment framework and consistent reporting format need to be developed and systematically applied in Latvia. Then, these frameworks should be used to inform decision making. The challenge looks to be less about improving the data infrastructure itself, but more about putting in place tools and structures that help make the Latvian NHS a data-driven system. OECD countries offer some examples that Latvia could follow, for example dashboards of core quality and performance indicators available at a national and/or local and/or hospital level. In Scotland the LDP (Local Delivery Plan) standards are used both to set health policy, to monitor performance and progress against set expectations, and assess local performance (Box 2.10). In Tuscany, Italy, a measurement framework has been developed for the Tuscan Local Health Authority which has since been adopted by other health regions, is as an internal evaluation tool for performance and quality. The performance evaluation programme (see Box 2.11) includes a range of quality indicators recognised by international organisations including the OECD, WHO and the EU Commission through the European Community Health Indicators (ECHI).

Box 2.10. Local Delivery Plan (LPD) Standards in Scotland

The second level of the Quality Measurement Framework is made up of a suite of national NHS performance targets that NHSScotland and the Scottish Government agree to each year. They are known as Local Delivery Plan (LDP) Standards and cover traditional performance targets such as emergency department attendances and smoking cessation, alongside more innovative measures such as sickness absence of NHS staff (believed to be important because of the impact on cancelled appointments and procedures, leading to increased pressure on staff and patients, increased costs of employing bank and agency staff, and reduced efficiency). The inclusion of this target helps underline the need to see a whole-system approach to targets and system performance relative to targets, considering the inputs and drivers behind successfully, or unsuccessfully, met targets.

As for the indicators linked to the National Performance Framework, performance against the LDP Standards is reported online. Importantly, an explanation of why a particular target is used aims to help staff and patient understanding, and is provided alongside the LDP Standard results on the NHSScotland website.

Table 2.3. Standards to measure Scottish health system performance (selected)

	LDP standard
Detect cancer early	Increase the proportion of people diagnosed and treated in the first stage of breast, colorectal and lung cancer by 25%.
Cancer waiting times	95% of all patients diagnosed with cancer to begin treatment within 31 days of decision to treat, and 95% of those referred urgently with a suspicion of cancer to begin treatment within 62 days of receipt of referral.
Treatment time guarantee	100% of patients to wait no longer than 12 weeks from the patient agreeing treatment with the hospital to treatment for inpatient or day case treatment.
18 weeks referral-to-treatment	90% of planned / elective patients to commence treatment within 18 weeks of referral.
Psychological therapies waiting times	90% of patients to commence psychological therapy based treatment within 18 weeks of referral.
Staph. aureus bacteraemia (MRSA/MSSA)	NHS Boards' rate of SAB (staphylococcus aureus bacteraemia (including MRSA)) cases are 0.24 or less per 1 000 acute occupied bed days.
Smoking cessation	NHS Boards to sustain and embed successful smoking quits at 12 weeks post quit, in the 40% most deprived SIMD areas (60% in the Island Boards).
GP access	GPs to provide 48-hour access or advance booking to an appropriate member of the GP team for at least 90% of patients.
Sickness absence	NHS Boards to achieve a sickness absence rate of 4% or less.
Accident and emergency waiting times	95% of patients to wait no longer than 4 hours from arrival to admission, discharge or transfer for A&E treatment. Boards to work towards 98%.
Financial performance	NHS Boards are required to operate within their Revenue Resource Limit (RRL), their Capital Resource Limit (CRL) and meet their Cash Requirement.

Source: Scotland Performs: NHSScotland, available at: http://www.gov.scot/About/Performance/scotPerforms/partnerstories/NHSScotlandperformance, accessed 18.10.2015.

Box 2.11. The Tuscan Performance Evaluation Programme

The Tuscan Performance Evaluation Programme is an innovative measurement framework used as an internal evaluation tool for health care organisation. It was developed in 2005 to measure the quality of health care services in order to improve population health and to achieve higher quality of life. At present, the system is implemented in eight other Italian regions. It gathers more than 130 indicators, classified in six dimensions: population health status, capacity to pursue regional strategies, clinical performance, patient satisfaction, staff satisfaction and efficiency or financial performance. The performance results are monitored every three months with feedbacks provided to health care professionals and managers. They are also linked to the CEOs' reward system and made publicly available. Available evidence suggested that more than 50% of the indicators significantly improved in Toscana between 2006 and 2010 (Nuti et al., 2013), leading to better quality of care and increasing both population health and quality of life.

Although the Tuscan performance management system is perhaps the system most familiar to non-Italian health system researchers, it should be stressed that in Italy it is viewed as one of a number of equally valid approaches being developed by different regions.

Source: OECD (2014), *OECD Reviews of Health Care Quality: Italy – Raising Standards*, OECD Publishing, Paris, http://dx.doi.org/10.1787/9789264225428-en.

Latvia could become a more data-driven system, with a richer data infrastructure including provider-level reporting, which is more systematically used for decision making

Latvia could stand to become a more-data driven health system, in terms of both available data, and the way that data is used. Developing more complete, more granular and better linked provider-data systems will be the first step for Latvia in more fully addressing efficiency, waste, and care quality. In a resource-stretched country like Latvia not only can such advances in data exploitation bring greater value for money from spending, but it is also very likely a less costly way of promoting quality than some other possible quality levers, for instance resource-intensive accreditation or clinical audit programmes.

Provider-level reporting has contributed to improved quality of care across countries, and Latvia could certainly consider reporting provider performance more consistently. Provider-level data, in particular, would help Latvia understand differences in quality and efficiency between providers. For instance, one of the things that would help Latvia understand why case-fatality rates are so much higher than OECD countries (for AMI and stroke, see Section 2.3) would be more granular data at the provider level. This would show first whether case fatality was poor across the hospital sector or whether there are some better performing hospitals, second, to allow lessons from better performing hospitals to be spread whilst directing support to poorer-performing providers, and third, monitor the impact of initiatives introduced to improve quality and efficiency at the provider level.

Latvia will also need to more systematically and extensively draw on health system data to inform decision making and performance and quality assessments, at all levels of the health system. Countries like Sweden, Canada and Portugal (see Box 2.12) all have well-developed health data infrastructures, where data is regularly reported and used as part of decision making at national, local, provider level and patient level.

Box 2.12. Data driven health care systems in OECD countries

Monitoring health system performance in Sweden

The National Board of Health and Welfare and the Swedish Association of Local Authorities and Regions (SALAR) regularly publish counties' performance across more than 150 indicators of health care in its *Quality and Efficiency in Swedish Health Care report.* These include measures of access (such as ambulance response time, availability of primary care by phone), effectiveness (such as implant survival after hip replacement or meeting rehabilitation needs after stroke), safety (such as polypharmacy rates in the elderly or hospital acquired infection) and patient experience (such as reported respect and consideration in primary care or holding of end of life conversations). Efficiency measures are included in the same publication, such as cost per contact within the primary care system and cost per DRG point produced in hospitals. Data are presented for both local health authorities as well as individual clinics and hospitals.

Monitoring health system performance in Canada

The Canadian Institute for Health Information consolidates and publishes health system performance data on the yourhealthsystem.cihi.ca website. Simple definitions of technical terms (such as "Getting needed care at the right time, without financial, organisational or geographical barriers" for access) and questions (such as "Are Canadians actually getting healthier?") are the predominant tools used to guide users around the website. The *In Brief* section of the website focuses on five themes that prior research revealed were of most interest to Canadians: access, quality, spending, prevention and outcomes. The *In Depth* section uses 37 indicators to go into more detail, as well as providing descriptive data of health service resources and activity. The indicators in this section cover all dimensions of health system performance, including quality (such as readmission rates or restraint use in long-term care), efficiency (such as the cost of a standard hospital stay), access (such as waiting times for emergency physician assessment) and prevention (such as smoking and obesity rates). Results are available by province, territory, region, city or hospital and infographics are used to convey statistical information, including benchmarking against regional and national averages.

Sundhed.dk, the Danish e-health portal

Sundhed.dk, the Danish e-health portal, is the official portal for the public Danish health care services and enables patients and health care professionals to find information and communicate. Denmark has been at the forefront on many IT initiatives within health services. Sundhed.dk is a public, internet-based portal that collects and distributes health care information among citizens and health care professionals. In a secure part of the portal the patient has access to:

- Personal health data on treatments and notes from hospital records, information about medication and visits to the GP;
- Various e-services including making appointments with GP's, prescription renewals and electronic communication with the GP;
- Information on waiting times at all public hospitals and ratings of hospitals in terms of patient experienced quality;
- Patient networks and the sundhed.dk handbook for patients.

It is unique in bringing the entire Danish health care sector together on the Internet and providing an accessible setting for citizens and health care professionals to meet and efficiently exchange information. By servicing both the citizens and the health professionals, the portals aim is to enable the two to achieve co-operation based on the same data. This should empower the citizen and gives the health professionals better tools to improve quality in care (OECD, 2013c).

Box 2.12. Data driven health care systems in OECD countries *(cont.)*

An integrated data platform for policy, practitioners and patients in Portugal

Portugal has an extensive information infrastructure which – relatively exceptionally – spans almost all levels of care, and this data is also in many instances actively used to drive quality improvements. Data sources include setting specific information structures, and disease-specific registers and data sources. Much of Portugal's rich data infrastructure is thanks to the use of electronic patient records and unique patient identifiers. These records go towards creating the Portuguese Health Data Platform (PDS), which consists of a Patient Portal (Portal Do Utente, launched May 2012), a Professional Portal (Portal Do Professional, launched June 2012), an Institutional Portal (Portal Institucional, under testing) and an International Portal (Portal Internacional, piloted June 2013). The different portals hold different information, to be used in different ways. For instance, the Professional Portal provides health professionals with patient clinical data and records stored from different institutions and central repositories. The Institutional Portal, when operational, should provide statistics from anonymised clinical data to central institutions.

Eventually, PDS is intended to be a platform linking together data from across the health system. Prescriptions, a chronic kidney disease register, a surgical safety checklist, and birth reports are all, for example, included in PDS. Long-term care, an often neglected area of data collection, is also included in PDS using the RNCCI database. The PDS database consists of several application modules that allow the recording of: medical, nursing, and social service evaluations; assessment by other professionals (rehabilitation medicine, physiotherapy, psychology, occupational therapy, etc.); IAI, a bio-psychosocial evaluation method; pressure ulcer risk evaluation and recording; falls risk evaluation; health care associated infections; pain evaluation; discharge abstracts; diabetes assessment; adverse drug reaction notification; and acute exacerbations.

Nonetheless, not all of Portugal's rich data can be linked together or accessed from all health care services, and in practice patients cannot easily be followed across care settings.

Source: OECD (2013), *OECD Reviews of Health Care Quality: Denmark – Raising Standards*, OECD Publishing, Paris, http://dx.doi.org/10.1787/9789264191136-en; OECD (2013), *OECD Reviews of Health Care Quality: Sweden 2013 – Raising Standards*, OECD Publishing, Paris, http://dx.doi.org/10.1787/9789264204799-en; OECD (2015), *OECD Reviews of Health Care Quality: Portugal 2015 – Raising Standards*, OECD Publishing, Paris, http://dx.doi.org/10.1787/9789264225985-en.

Sustainable development of human resources in the health sector

Based on more data on health professionals and their estimated demand, Latvia needs a mix of measures to develop and adequately distribute human resources, to tackle the foreseen shortage of certain health professionals, and to develop human resource skills. The existing shape of the Latvian workforce, which is set out in Chapter 1, presents a number of challenges, including the geographic distribution of health professionals, the ageing workforce, the challenge of low salaries and out-migration of health professionals, and of the need for the workforce to adapt to meet changing population health needs.

Approaches to addressing workforce challenges could be brought together in a comprehensive workforce plan (see Section 2.6). Such a plan should consider training needs, based on expected retirement rates. Geographical shortages of health professionals should be considered, and Latvia could consider targeting recruitment for training towards populations in rural and under-served areas who may be more likely to wish to return to practice in the area (see Section 2.2). Financial incentives for physicians, nurses, pharmacists and other health professionals to serve in rural areas could be again considered, although so far higher salaries in rural areas does not appear to have encouraged specialists to re-locate. Other incentives, such as access to a broader range of services such as accommodation and child care, may prove more attractive. Additionally, an obligatory rotation, or incentive package, to work in a rural or remote area immediately post-qualification has been introduced in countries such as France, Australia or Belgium, and could be considered in Latvia.

In terms of considering ways to strengthen and grow Latvia's workforce, reflection on remuneration and working conditions – particularly for nurses – will likely need consideration. Latvia's nurses have some of the lowest salaries in the OECD – and, with an important impact on nurses out-migration and retention, in the European Union. To keep nurses (and doctors) in Latvia, and in the nursing profession, higher salaries, and more scope to take on additional tasks and responsibilities, may well be needed. The European Union has so far played an important role in providing financial support for training of health professionals and also to ameliorate the geographic distribution of doctors, but Latvia will also likely need to commit more financial resources to the medical workforce to ensure sufficient staffing levels, and promote workforce quality.

Appropriate ways of expanding professional roles to meet changing needs, and maximising workforce contribution, should also be considered. For example pharmacists could contribute more to care for patients with chronic conditions in the community, and the role of nurses could be expanded into areas such as prevention and health promotion (Chapter 3). However, in the Public Health Strategy for 2014-20 a number of activities are planned for strengthening the role of primary health care professionals in health promotion and prevention. Already some efforts to increase the contribution of the nursing workforce have been considered, but reports suggest that logistical challenges – such as the unavailability of a second practice room for nurses to work out of – is limiting the impact of this change (see also Chapter 3).

Finally, ways to improve and maintain workforce quality should be included in any workforce planning. This should include appropriate professional regulatory frameworks, as well as quality improvement efforts such as continuing professional development requirements and/or incentives. Re-certification has been in place in Latvia for 20 years, marking the country out as a front-runner in the international trend towards re-certification. As well as assuring quality of professionals, it is understood that the re-certification requirement contributes to quality of CPD in the country; in the most part health care employers pay for this compulsory training, although in some cases, individuals have to pay. Given that Latvia already has a well-established history of re-certification and CPD, a potential workforce strategy should include recognition of this, and a scoping exercise to ensure that CPD and re-certification coverage is appropriate (i.e. across the right range of health care professions, including nurses, physician's assistants).

Long-term care needs to be adequately developed

In a society with a large share of the elderly, there is also a large demand for long-term care but this sector has not been developed adequately in Latvia. Latvia will need to explore strategies for coping with changing population needs in a sustainable way. Although municipalities are responsible for assuring access to long-term care to the local population through securing long-term care services provided at hospitals and providing social services in institutions and home care with health professionals and social workers, the quality and availability of LTC vary across municipalities, so national strategies are needed to organise the delivery of LTC and also care co-ordination across different care settings and function of care more systematically, and in a more consistent and enduring way.

Family carers are the backbone of any LTC system. Supporting family carers effectively is important as high-intensity care giving is associated with a reduction in labour supply for paid work, a higher risk of poverty, and a 20% higher prevalence of mental health problems among family carers than for non-carers. Supporting family carers is beneficial for care recipients, because they generally prefer to be looked after by family and friends. And it is also beneficial for public finances, because it involves far less public expenditure for a given amount of care than if it was provided in the formal sector. Governments can support family carers by providing cash, promoting more choice and flexibility, for example through care leave, and introducing support services such as respite care, training and counselling. Both carers' allowances and cash benefits paid to the care recipients, in the Nordic and all English-speaking countries, has increased the supply of family care. Flexible work arrangements in the United Kingdom, Australia and the United States attenuate the risk of a reduction in working hours associated with caring. Support services, which can be arranged for a relatively low cost, ensure quality of care as carers' wellbeing is improved.

Most OECD governments have set up collectively-financed schemes for personal and nursing-care costs. One third of the countries have universal coverage either as part of a tax-funded social-care system, as in Nordic countries, or through dedicated social insurance schemes, as in Germany, Japan, Korea, Netherlands and Luxembourg, or by arranging coverage mostly within the health system, as in Belgium. While not having a dedicated "LTC system", several countries have universal personal-care benefits, whether in cash (e.g., Austria, France, Italy) or in kind (e.g., Australia, New Zealand). Finally, two countries have "safety net" or means-tested schemes for LTC costs, namely the United Kingdom (excluding Scotland, which has a universal system) and the United States (Colombo et al., 2011).

Moving towards universal LTC benefits is desirable on access grounds. Uncertainty with respect to whether, when, and for how long an individual might need LTC services suggests that pooling the financial risk associated with long-term care is a more efficient solution than relying on out-of-pocket payments. Otherwise, the cost of LTC services and support is unaffordable for most people. However, to maintain control over expenditure, it is important to implement target universal care benefits where needs are the highest and move towards forward-looking financing policies. Japan, the Netherlands, Belgium and Luxembourg complement payroll contributions with alternative revenue sources. In Germany, retirees are required to contribute premia to social LTC funds, as well as those of working age. Innovative voluntary funding schemes based on automatic enrolment with opting-out options exist in Singapore and are being implemented in the United States (Colombo et al., 2011).

Notes

1. *Note by Turkey*: The information in this report with reference to "Cyprus" relates to the southern part of the Island. There is no single authority representing both Turkish and Greek Cypriot people on the Island. Turkey recognises the Turkish Republic of Northern Cyprus (TRNC). Until a lasting and equitable solution is found within the context of the United Nations, Turkey shall preserve its position concerning the "Cyprus issue".

2. *Note by all the European Union Member States of the OECD and the European Union*: The Republic of Cyprus is recognised by all members of the United Nations with the exception of Turkey. The information in this report relates to the area under the effective control of the Government of the Republic of Cyprus.

References

CDPC (2013), "Database of Hospital Beds' Utilisation and Database of Out-Patient Care Usage", Centre for Disease Prevention and Control, Riga.

Colombo, F. et al. (2011), *Help Wanted? Providing and Paying for Long-Term Care*, Publishing, Paris, http://dx.doi.org/10.1787/9789264097759-en

EU-SILC (2013), http://ec.europa.eu/eurostat/statistics-explained/index.php/Glossary:EU_statistics_on_income_and_living_conditions_(EU-SILC)/fr.

European Commission (2014), *Special Eurobarometer 411: Patient Safety and Quality of Care*, Conducted by TNS Opinion & Social.

Ministry of Finance of the Republic of Latvia (2014), "Public Health Strategy for 2014-2020", adopted by the Cabinet of Ministers on October 14, 2014 by order No. 589.

Mitenbergs, U. et al. (2012), "Latvia: Health System Review", *Health Systems in Transition*, Vol. 14, No. 8, pp. 1-191.

OECD (2015a), *OECD Reviews of Health Care Quality: Australia 2015: Raising Standards*, OECD Publishing, Paris, http://dx.doi.org/10.1787/9789264233836-en.

OECD (2015b), *OECD Reviews of Health Care Quality: Japan 2015: Raising Standards*, OECD Publishing, Paris, http://dx.doi.org/10.1787/9789264225817-en.

OECD (2015c), *OECD Reviews of Health Care Quality: Portugal 2015: Raising Standards*, OECD Publishing, Paris, http://dx.doi.org/10.1787/9789264225985-en.

OECD (2015d), "Focus on Health Spending: OECD Health Statistics 2015", OECD, Paris, available at: http://www.oecd.org/health/health-systems/Focus-Health-Spending-2015.pdf.

OECD (2015e), *Cardiovascular Disease and Diabetes: Policies for Better Health and Quality of Care*, OECD Publishing, Paris, http://dx.doi.org/10.1787/9789264233010-en.

OECD (2015f), *OECD Health Statistics 2015*, http://dx.doi.org/10.1787/health-data-en.

OECD (2014a), *Health at a Glance: Europe 2014*, OECD Publishing, Paris, http://dx.doi.org/10.1787/health_glance_eur-2014-en.

OECD (2014b), *OECD Reviews of Health Care Quality: Norway: Raising Standards*, OECD Publishing, Paris, http://dx.doi.org/10.1787/9789264208605-en.

OECD (2014c), *Geographic Variations in Health Care: What Do We Know and What Can Be Done to Improve Health System Performance?*, OECD Publishing, Paris, http://dx.doi.org/10.1787/9789264216594-en.

OECD (2014d), *OECD Reviews of Health Care Quality: Italy: Raising Standards*, OECD Publishing, Paris, http://dx.doi.org/10.1787/9789264225428-en.

OECD (2014e), *Making Mental health Count: The Social and Economic Costs of Neglecting Mental Health Care*, OECD Publishing, Paris, http://dx.doi.org/10.1787/9789264208445-en.

OECD (2013a), *OECD Reviews of Health Care Quality: Denmark: Raising Standards*, OECD Publishing, Paris, http://dx.doi.org/10.1787/9789264191136-en.

OECD (2013b), *OECD Reviews of Health Care Quality: Sweden 2013: Raising Standards*, OECD Publishing, Paris, http://dx.doi.org/10.1787/9789264204799-en.

OECD (2013c), *Cancer Care: Assuring Quality to Improve Survival*, OECD Publishing, Paris, http://dx.doi.org/10.1787/9789264181052-en.

OECD/European Commission (2013), *A Good Life in Old Age? Monitoring and Improving Quality in Long-term Care*, OECD Publishing, Paris, http://dx.doi.org/10.1787/9789264194564-en.

Scotland Performs: NHSScotland (2015), http://www.gov.scot/About/Performance/scotPerforms/partnerstories/NHSScotlandperformance, accessed 18 October 2015.

Siciliani, L., M. Borowitz and V. Moran (eds.) (2013c), *Waiting Time Policies in the Health Sector: What Works?*, OECD Publishing, Paris, http://dx.doi.org/10.1787/9789264179080-en.

World Bank (2012), "Implementation Completion and Results Report on a Series of Two Loans to the Republic of Latvia for a Safety Net and Social Sector Reform Program", http://documents.worldbank.org/curated/en/2012/06/16518638/latvia-safety-net-social-sector-reform-program-project.

World Bank (2015), "The Active Aging Challenge for Longer Working Lives in Latvia", http://pubdocs.worldbank.org/en/205791443642635843/WB-Latvia-Active-Aging-Report.pdf.

Chapter 3

Strengthening primary health care in Latvia

A strong, well-established primary care sector is one of the Latvian health system's key attributes. Good accessibility, patient registration and smart regulation around staff mix mean that Latvian general practitioners are well placed to offer proactive, co-ordinated care for an ageing population. In addition, an intelligently designed payment system and an incipient quality-monitoring framework mark out primary care as an ambitious and forward-looking sector capable of delivering substantial value for money.

Closer integration with other parts of the health system is needed, however. A substantial disconnect still characterises relations between primary and secondary care and mechanisms are needed to allow GPs to stay involved across a patient's entire pathway of care. Primary and secondary prevention are far from adequate, and Latvian GPs will need to deliver considerably improved care in these areas. Once the quality-monitoring framework for GPs is better established, it should focus on clinical outcomes rather than activities to support them to deliver better care.

The statistical data for Israel are supplied by and under the responsibility of the relevant Israeli authorities. The use of such data by the OECD is without prejudice to the status of the Golan Heights, East Jerusalem and Israeli settlements in the West Bank under the terms of international law.

Introduction

There is growing recognition among policy makers that a strong primary health care system is the foundation of a health system that is effective, efficient and responsive to patients' needs. Latvia is moving in that direction with a Primary Health Care Development Plan that strives to improve quality and accessibility of health services, and enhances preventive activities to keep people out of more expensive hospital care.

Fully capitalising on the plan will require a payment system that motivates general practitioners (GPs) to improve the quality of care they deliver to patients, and to participate more proactively in preventive tasks such as cancer screening. Latvia has demonstrated that it can use its workforce innovatively to improve access to primary care, but needs to strengthen the role that GPs and other health care professionals play in health promotion, particularly educating patients about chronic disease self-management.

This chapter is configured as follows. Section 3.1 describes the structure of the Latvian primary health care system, and workforce and other challenges. Section 3.2 surveys reforms to primary care in Latvia, including a performance framework that aims to drive improvements in quality. Section 3.3 assesses the performance of the primary health care system, and how Latvia fares on a range of indicators. Section 3.4 sets out recommendations to strengthen primary health care in Latvia.

3.1. The structure of primary health care in Latvia

GPs are a strong feature of the Latvian primary health care system, although workforce shortages particularly in rural areas are a challenge. Despite registration with a family doctor being voluntary, most Latvians choose to sign up with one practice. GPs act as health-system gatekeepers, providing referrals for patients to visit most specialists. To prepare itself for both an ageing population and GP workforce, Latvia has endeavoured to improve primary care access with the creation of second practice nurse and physician assistant roles.

General practitioner numbers are small in Latvia, particularly in rural areas

While the number of GPs in Latvia has grown in recent years, the numbers are still small compared with other European countries. In 2013, there were 67 generalist medical practitioners per 100 000 population in Latvia, a significant rise compared with 45 per 100 000 population a decade earlier. However, when compared with neighbouring countries Lithuania (92) and Estonia (89), the Latvian GP numbers are modest (Eurostat, 2015a). Despite this, independent GP practices are a strong feature of the Latvian primary health care system. Providers contracting with the Latvian National Health Service (NHS) may be public or private, and tend to be mostly private in the case of primary care.

The NHS has an established network of GP practices with which it has contracts either with single GP practices or – if GPs provide services as employees of health centres or hospital outpatient departments – with the administration of the institution. There are targets for the number of GPs contracted in a region, and newly certified GPs are placed on a waiting list to be contracted or can apply for very limited vacancies. The number of physicians without a contract is small. Patients who choose an uncontracted GP have to cover all costs of the services according to the GP's price list.

In common with many OECD countries, the geographical distribution of GP practices in Latvia is uneven. The capital Riga accounts for 37% of practices, while 15% are in the

Greater Riga Area (Pierīga), 14% are in Latgale, 13% in Kurzeme, 12% in Zemgale and 10% in Vidzeme. While this distribution generally corresponds to that of the population size, primary care accessibility weakens with increasing distance from the capital.

Barriers to opening new practices in rural areas include the spread of residents across large areas and the unwillingness of GPs to move to these areas, partly due to professional isolation. Adding to the challenge is that GPs often serve as providers of secondary care due to a lack of specialists in rural areas. Latvia has tried to deal with these issues by providing financial incentives for GPs in rural areas to maintain at least a second practice, to increase access across different locations. To receive these payments, GPs must see patients at the secondary sites at least weekly. To encourage new GPs to work in rural areas, doctors contracted with the NHS receive a fixed bonus for maintaining a practice and employing staff in rural areas. The bonus is based on the density of the population in a given area, and the number of registered patients. Medical residents working outside of Riga receive 30% higher salaries than those working in Riga.

To practise, GPs are required to obtain 250 credits of continuing medical education (CME) within a five-year period. To be recertified, they must have worked in their specialty for at least three of the previous five years. If re-certification is denied, for example due to insufficient CME credits, the GP must take the re-certification examination.

Most Latvians are registered with a named GP

Almost all the Latvian population is registered with a GP, despite the fact that registration is voluntary. Registration with a practice has been shown to help ensure continuity of patient care, particularly if the GP adopts the role of care co-ordinator for patients with chronic disease. Latvians can freely choose their GP, and there are no restrictions around how often they change their GP. However, there are defined catchment areas, and a GP is entitled to refuse to register a patient if they live outside their catchment area, or if the GP already has 1 800 registered adult patients or 800 children, unless the patient's close relatives are already registered with the practice.

As of 31 December 2013, the NHS had contracts with 1 365 GPs, serving more than 2 million registered patients. However, the GP workload varies broadly. On average, there were 1 561 patients registered with each GP in 2013. In the case of about 10% of GP practices, the number of registered patients is considered insufficient. By contrast, for almost 15% of GPs, the number of registered patients exceeds 2 000. There are examples of practices with registered patient numbers exceeding 2 800.

Patients have the freedom to choose their own doctor, and this choice is one that Latvians seem to value. If a GP ceases to practise, patients are informed about the possibility of registering with other GPs, including with the GP who is taking over the practice. An analysis of data on transferred GP practices indicates that on average, more than three-quarters of patients at a particular practice choose to register with the incoming GP, while the others register with a different GP. In some practices, a different GP is chosen by almost half of patients, demonstrating the ability to freely change their GP is important to the public.

Most Latvian GPs work in solo practices. This lies in contrast to many OECD countries, where there has been a shift towards larger teams in recognition of the economic and communal benefits of working with peers. In urban areas, many Latvian GPs work alongside other GPs in health centres. However, these are not group practices;

the GPs work individually and share the health centre infrastructure. Some GPs locate their practices near one another to share administrative and other costs, such as equipment, although this is not common practice.

The cost of rent is high, and a survey by the Latvian Association of General Practitioners indicates that 40% of general practices are in premises less than 40 m^2. In the capital of Riga, the proportion rises to 64%. This lack of space limits the capacity of GPs to provide a full variety of services. This is particularly important given that only 20% of GPs perform at least 30% of procedures available under their professional competence, according to the Annual Quality Assessment of GPs in Latvia (Table 3.1).

The Latvian Primary Health Care Development Plan (Box 3.3) cites GPs reporting that funding does not correspond with the reality of necessary costs for practices to provide effective services. Additionally, GPs face a high administrative burden which not only reduces clinical time with their patients, but adds an extra financial cost. Given the high cost of rent and other expenses, it has been reported that some GPs are taking up free premises in pharmacies.

Patients with referrals from a GP can choose any ambulatory or inpatient provider that has a contract with the NHS. Health centres are the most important providers of secondary ambulatory care, and employ specialists as well as GPs. About 70% to 80% of health centres are private, mostly in the capital of Riga, while the remaining are owned by municipalities. Local municipal hospitals are also providers of secondary outpatient care (Mitenbergs et al., 2012).

GPs perform the function of gatekeepers to the health system, providing referrals to specialists and hospital care. Such a system can help to facilitate feedback between providers. However, as discussed in Chapter 1, electronic health has not been fully implemented in Latvia, and communication between providers should improve once it is in operation. Some specialists do not require a referral from a GP. Latvian patients with a range of long-term conditions may go directly to a specialist without a referral from their GP in the following cases:

- psychiatrists: if a patient has a psychiatric disorder;
- endocrinologists: if a patient has diabetes;
- dermatovenereologists: if a patient has a sexually transmissible infection;
- addiction specialists: if a patient has an addiction to alcohol, narcotics or psychotropics;
- infectious disease specialists: if a patient has HIV;
- gynaecologists;
- ophthalmologists;
- paediatric surgeons;
- paediatricians;
- sports doctors;
- pulmonologists: if a patient has tuberculosis;
- oncologists and oncological chemotherapists: if a patient has an oncological illness.

With Latvia's population ageing, it is likely that more of the population will have multiple morbidities. Patients with chronic disease should ideally be managed by a multidisciplinary team, with GPs co-ordinating the care of patients. However, the current system in Latvia that enables patients to see specialists without a referral – even in limited circumstances – does not support GPs to take on this role. Additionally, some of the care that patients seek directly from a specialist could be managed by a GP, adding an unnecessary cost to the system. This is particularly the case for gynaecologists. In many countries, cervical cancer screening is considered a routine task performed in general practice. However, Latvian GPs do not perform this role.

Making GPs the first point of contact for patients, providing referrals to specialists if necessary, presents both efficiency and quality gains. Many countries, such as Australia, the United Kingdom and The Netherlands, emphasise the role of the GP as the gatekeeper to the health system. Portugal has a strong primary health care system and emphasises the role of the GP as gatekeeper and care co-ordinator. Portuguese GPs are also heavily involved in health promotion and preventive work. The primary health care model adopted by Portugal (Box 3.1) is one that Latvia and other countries could learn from.

Box 3.1. Family Health Units in Portugal

The primary care system in Portugal is the first port of call for patients with non-emergency concerns. Most services are carried out by GPs, assisted by nurses and other health professionals. Access to hospitals and publically-covered specialist services is controlled by gatekeeping at the primary care level. Portugal has two models in the primary care system.

Primary Health Care Units (PHCUs) are essentially clinic settings that group together varying numbers of GPs, who provide care to their patient list. They vary in structure and size. Staff are paid based on a fixed salary basis.

Family Health Units (FHUs) are primary health care units made up of three to eight GPs, the same number of family nurses, and a variable number of administrative staff, who were invited to volunteer to form self-selecting groups to deliver primary care together.

While the traditional working style in primary care is of GPs operating relatively independently, FHUs were intended to encourage more multidisciplinary team work. The average FHU has around 12 000 patients, seven doctors and 20 professionals in total. These teams have functional and technical autonomy and a payment system sensitive to performance that is designed to reward productivity, accessibility and quality, with core indicators used to measure performance. Staff are salaried, with a performance-based payment component.

Source: OECD (2015), *OECD Reviews of Health Care Quality: Portugal 2015: Raising Standards*, OECD Publishing, Paris, http://dx.doi.org/10.1787/9789264225985-en.

Payment to GPs includes a pay-for-performance scheme that aims to drive improvements in quality

Payments to Latvian GPs are made up of a number of elements. A payment is calculated based on the number of registered patients, with a capitation amount adjusted for age and coefficient of consumption of family doctor services. However, it is not clear which primary care services are covered in the capitation payment. Additionally, GPs receive other payments for medical procedures they perform, such as those related to vaccinations and preventive check-ups.

There are also monthly fixed payments to general practices. Additionally, there are a number of monthly fixed bonuses for maintaining and employing staff in rural areas, compliance of the age structure of the registered patients to the type of family doctor practice, and for treating chronic patients. A compulsory pay-for-performance scheme, introduced in 2013, aims to drive quality improvements. GPs who fulfil quality criteria can earn financial bonuses, payable once per year. This is discussed further in Section 3.2.

Other ways GPs can earn additional income aim to encourage them to engage in good clinical practice. To reduce unnecessary referrals for laboratory tests, GPs receive a payment if laboratory referrals are no less than 80%, but do not exceed more than 100%, of the amount set for the GP for the previous year. In addition, to promote the early diagnosis of cancer, GPs can receive payments of EUR 71.14 per patient to detect first and second-stage cancer in their registered patients. This is an important incentive but, as discussed in Section 3.3, it is unclear how effective it is given cancer screening is very low in Latvia.

GPs can also generate additional income by providing paid services, such as home visits for patient groups for whom such visits are not paid for by the state. They can receive additional payments from the NHS for treating patients not registered at their practice, payments for nurses and physician assistants (Box 3.2), and remuneration for substituting another family doctor if it is for a period of more than two months. Patients visiting a GP must make a co-payment of EUR 1.42, although exemptions apply for children, pregnant women and the poor. In these cases, the contributions are covered by the state.

The Health Inspectorate supervises quality and safety in primary health care

The Health Inspectorate ensures that GPs provide safe and high-quality care in accordance with regulations, and can impose penalties where irregularities are identified. Health Inspectorate data indicate that not all general practices and dental surgeries meet these requirements. In 2012, there were 263 planned and unplanned inspections regarding the implementation of requirements for GPs, of which 205 (78%) established various irregularities. Penalties were imposed in five cases.

The most commonly detected irregularities in general practice range from necessary information not indicated in medical documents, to not providing an accessible environment for people with disabilities. Prolonged waiting times for urgent patients, inappropriately prescribing medication, "unreasonably" refusing state-paid home visits, and not organising the workplace for a second practice nurse are other issues.

In 2012, there were also 123 inspections of GPs with regards to the use of state-funded budget and organisation of practice work. Irregularities were established in 109 cases (87%). There were also 121 inspections regarding practices meeting provisions in the legislation. In these cases, 98 (81%) irregularities were established and penalties were imposed in seven (6%) cases. Penalties include written warnings and fines.

The Latvian GP workforce is ageing, and practice nurses and physician assistants are part of the plan to improve access

In addition to the geographical distribution of GPs posing challenges for Latvia, the country's ageing workforce will also make access to primary care more difficult for patients. The average age of GPs is 54, making workforce succession planning a priority. More than two-thirds of practising GPs are aged 50 and over, and more than a quarter are aged 60 and over (CDPC, 2014). Latvia is already beginning to recognise these issues in its planning of residency placements. In 2012, there were 22 residencies in family medicine, and the number grew to 28 in 2014. Still, there is scope to considerably increase these numbers.

In a bid to strengthen primary health care and cope with these access challenges, Latvia began financing a second nurse for general practices in 2010. Employing a second nurse or physician assistant (Box 3.2) became mandatory in 2014 for practices with more than 1 800 registered patients or 800 patients aged under 18. While there are sufficient numbers of nurses in large cities, employing nurses in rural areas has proven to be more difficult. Second general practice nurses focus on prevention, and are paid by the state if they work in practices with at least 1 200 patients. They are intended to discuss with patients life style risk factors such as smoking and harmful alcohol consumption. However, the extent to which they do this differs between practices. While they would be ideally placed to assist in co-ordinating the care of patients with chronic conditions, in reality they seldom perform this role. Given GPs engage in limited health promotion work with patients, second practice nurses could be upskilled to take on more of this role.

While second practice nurses have not yet realised their full potential, they have at least helped improve access to primary health care. Their role, and its potential expansion, could be one of interest to OECD countries. The number of GP practices funded to have a second practice nurse grew from 59 at the beginning of 2010 (their first year), to 288 at year's end. Given these nurses have at least ten hours a week of patient contact, they can be considered to have helped to improve access. To truly capitalise on their potential, however, second nurses should play a more prominent role in chronic disease management and preventive care.

Another important way Latvia is striving to improve access to primary health care is by creating the role of physician assistant (Box 3.2).

Box 3.2. Physician assistants in Latvia

The Latvian physician assistant (*feldsher*) plays an important role in general practice, particularly in areas where GPs are scarcer. Physician assistants are medical practitioners with a secondary professional education or the first level of higher professional education. They have two distinct roles, working either in ambulatory care or emergency departments.

In primary care, they provide health services to those with critical and life-threatening conditions. Their tasks can include providing first aid, administering vaccinations, carrying out home visits and issuing certificates for sickness-related absences from work. They work in health promotion, rehabilitation, diagnosis, treatment progress and patient education. They also implement the instructions of GPs and specialists. There were 96 such physician assistant practices in operation at the end of 2013, visited by patients on average 4.4 times per day.

In areas where access to health care is more challenging, local municipalities have established physician assistant units. To open such a unit, at least one of the following criteria must be met: the region in which the physician assistant unit is located is one without a registered GP practice; or the distance from the unit to the nearest GP practice is more than ten kilometres; or the area the unit serves has no fewer than 500 residents.

Physician assistants also provide medical assistance in emergency departments, working as part of a team and also in emergency call centres. Their tasks include diagnosis, assessment of condition severity, provision of treatment, and declaration of death. Physician assistants have the potential to take on a more prominent role in health care delivery, and Latvia should explore more innovative ways to use them.

There is also potential to enhance the role of Latvia's more than 1 600 pharmacists and more than 1 400 pharmaceutical assistants, who are an under-used resource in primary health care. Latvian pharmacists can provide pharmacotherapeutic consultations and information about medicine and its use. They can also supervise the use of medicine by permanent customers, and engage in some health promotion and disease prevention.

There could be scope Latvian pharmacists to take on a greater role. For example, in some parts of Australia, pharmacists are permitted to administer influenza and other vaccinations. In England, community pharmacists can participate in "minor ailment schemes", allowing patients to visit a pharmacy for treatment for limited conditions without the need to obtain a prescription from a GP. The aim of such schemes is to provide patients with health care and avoid the need for unnecessary GP or emergency department visits. Given pharmacists are more accessible in Latvia, improving their use could help improve access to health care particularly in areas where GPs are scarcer, and also represent savings for the health system.

Latvian primary care is at the forefront of the challenges presented by an ageing population

Latvia's population is ageing, making strengthening the country's primary health care system all the more crucial. This trend is partly explained by the fact that Latvia's population is also getting smaller, due to low fertility and high emigration of the younger population since the country's European Union accession.

Latvia's shrinking population is in common with Lithuania, Bulgaria, Romania, Estonia and Croatia. In 2012, those aged 50 and older accounted for 38.6% of Latvia's population. This is projected to grow to 45.6% in 2030. During the same period, the proportion aged 65 and over is projected to grow from 18.6% to 25.3% (World Bank, 2015).

Population ageing is inevitably accompanied by more chronic disease, and Latvia is already moving in the direction of strengthening primary health care to cope with these challenges. If Latvia is to be well-positioned to deal with this, however, there will need to be a stronger emphasis on patients seizing ownership of their own health care, and educating patients about self-management.

The country identified this problem in its Primary Health Care Development Plan 2014-16 (Box 3.3). The intention is to use information campaigns to increase public awareness and encourage people to take responsibility for their health. In this regard, Latvia has an opportunity to enhance the role of the second practice nurse, who is usually charged with the responsibility of informing patients about their condition. It is also the nurse's role to invite patients to come in for consultations. It is here that the nurse could play a more significant role in educating patients about their condition, and this would be all the more useful in the case of chronic disease.

The Plan also includes the introduction of group education organised by nurses and physician assistants at GP practices. Nurses at GP practices conduct health promotion and disease prevention activity in areas such as cardiovascular disease, perinatal and neonatal care and mental health care. Additionally, the Plan includes a course to improve teamwork in GP practices, in recognition of the fact that sometimes doctors do not divide responsibilities between themselves and nurses and physician assistants, and end up taking on responsibilities that could be delegated.

Latvia has acknowledged the need to rely less on more expensive hospital care. This began with the Development Programme for Outpatient and Inpatient Healthcare Service Providers in 2004. The programme's aim was to develop an integrated health care system and increase quality, accessibility and efficiency of the system. The plan included a reduction in hospital bed numbers to support the development of ambulatory care. Acute care bed numbers declined from 7 433 in 2010 to 6 748 in 2014, or from 35.4 to 33.8 per 10 000 population.

In common with many countries, Latvia implemented austerity measures during the economic crisis, including making cuts to the health budget. To avoid harming the most vulnerable populations, Latvia implemented the *Social Safety Net Strategy*. Its most important measure with respect to health was the exemption of needy and low-income people from user charges. These exemptions made it possible for socially disadvantaged people to receive free health care as long as they followed the normal patient pathway and obtained referrals from their GP for other services. However, in 2012, exemptions for low-income earners ceased, and applied only to needy people (Mitenbergs et al., 2012).

Other important measures in the *Social Safety Net Strategy* supported the shift away from hospital care to ambulatory care, with the aim of bolstering the care patients with chronic illness receive at home. This included free hotel-type accommodation for the poor, to reduce the need for patients to travel long distances to receive treatment. A home care service for the chronically ill was introduced, based on co-operation between GPs and home care providers – mostly the GP team with a nurse or a special home care team. Additionally, a telephone advisory service was developed to connect patients to a doctor to provide out-of-hours access (Mitenbergs et al., 2012).

Despite these measures, integrated care across the patient pathway is still in its infancy in Latvia. The need to improve care co-ordination, particularly for more vulnerable elderly people with multiple morbidities, remains a priority requiring attention.

3.2. Recent reforms

Latvia is striving to improve quality in primary care, through a range of quality indicators linked to a pay-for-performance scheme. There are questions, however, around the effectiveness of the scheme, particularly whether the quality bonuses are sufficient to incentivise doctors to drive quality improvements. Attempts are being made to improve the co-ordination of care across the patient pathway, although this work remains under-developed. The planned implementation of an electronic health system should go some way to improving the communication between health care providers.

Latvia's Primary Health Care Development Plan aims to improve access and quality, and increase the focus on prevention

As outlined in Chapter 1, the prevalence of risk factors such as smoking and alcohol is high in Latvia, and more focus should be given to reducing these risk factors that are associated with chronic disease. Latvia's Primary Health Care Development Plan includes a strengthened focus on health promotion and prevention, as well as treatment and rehabilitation (Box 3.3).

Box 3.3. Latvian Primary Health Care Development Plan 2014-16

The Primary Health Care Development Plan stresses that primary health care should be the first point of contact between an individual and the health system, as the basis of an efficient health care system. The plan intends to strengthen primary health care as the most accessible, effective and comprehensive level of care, by increasing the role of primary health care in prevention diagnostics and treatment, as well as improving quality of care. It says the aim of the plan will be reached if three courses of action are implemented: strengthening accessibility; improving quality and safety; and improving information assurance and compliance for patients. It sets out 12 "tasks" to achieve this, and accompanying activities:

1. To improve territorial availability of primary health care service providers – look at support mechanisms for GPs in areas with low population density; improve placement of medical centres; increase dental care availability.
2. To improve organisational availability of primary health care service providers – provide continuity of service support for GPs working alone; promote optimal number of patients registered with a practice; look at placement of doctors on duty and working time; improve documentation of medical files and other documents; and update the list of payable activities for GPs and dentists.
3. To improve requirements for primary health care service providers – develop criteria for selection of GPs for vacant places and for which state-funded dentistry services are chosen; assess opportunities to provide education for nurses and physician assistants.
4. To improve requirements for provided primary health care services – review and develop GPs' methodology for assessing annual activity and distribution of payment and their accounting system; improve the quality of telephone consultations.
5. To improve work organisation of primary health care service providers – increase e-health resource efficiency; strengthen GP teamwork in continuing professional development; review requirements for when a patient can go to a specialist without a GP referral.
6. To improve organisation and quality control of the provided primary health care services – increase efficiency and quality of inspections.
7. To increase the role of health promotion and disease prevention at the primary health care level – promote GP teamwork to follow up execution of preventive checks; increase colorectal cancer screening; improve GPs' epidemiological surveillance of communicable diseases and immunisation work; promote involvement of GPs, nurses and physician assistants in promoting physical activity in children.
8. To improve co-operation between primary health care service providers and other specialists – improve feedback and co-operation between specialists, patient organisations, GPs and dentists; improve co-operation between GPs and dentists for oral health promotion.
9. To improve the primary health care financing mechanism.
10. To improve and maintain information obtained about primary health care – study population satisfaction of primary health care in Latvia; develop information on dentistry.
11. To strengthen pharmaceutical care co-operation with primary health care – establish the role of pharmaceutical care to provide support for patients in self-care; improve patient health quality by providing consultations with clinical pharmacists about pharmacotherapy.
12. To inform the population about primary health care issues – improve information for patients about nearest service providers; organise public awareness activities for health promotion and disease prevention; begin programme of physician assistants providing education of patients in groups.

Comprehensive approaches involving a wide range of stakeholders, including GPs, are needed to promote healthy life styles

Given high prevalence and increasing rates of risk factors such as smoking and alcohol consumption, Latvia has taken measures to promote healthy life styles. While they have had some impact, they have not been strong enough to reverse the increasing prevalence of these risk factors. Latvia's health promotion activities include promoting healthy food particularly among school children, and active life styles. It has also conducted disease-specific programmes such as those targeting heart disease, cancer and HIV/AIDS.

Health promotion strategies require the involvement of different stakeholders, and the central government's leadership is key to developing comprehensive approaches to tackle unhealthy life styles. The focus of prevention and promotion of healthy life style in the current national health priorities will likely put more needed resources into this cost-saving health policy area which for years had not been given sufficient attention due to more emphasis on treating disease. This policy direction will also place more significance on prevention and health promotion within the Ministry of Health and Centre for Disease Prevention and Control, which need to play a major role in developing comprehensive strategies together with various stakeholders with different interests. Some OECD countries have adopted strong approaches to preventing disease (Box 3.4).

Box 3.4. Effective public health interventions across OECD countries

OECD countries have been making efforts to promote healthy life styles and positive impacts have been made in some areas. For example, tobacco control policies have been effective and have had a real impact on health outcomes in many OECD countries. Australia, Ireland, New Zealand, Turkey and the United Kingdom are among the countries with the most stringent and comprehensive set of anti-tobacco policies, including both population-wide measures and those targeting high-risk individuals through regulation, education, incentives, as well as health care programmes. Smoking rates in these countries have dropped more compared with countries with less stringent policies.

Alcohol policies should target heavy drinkers first. The OECD's economic analysis, focusing on Canada, the Czech Republic and Germany, shows that GPs can play an important role in addressing heavy drinking. Police enforcement of existing regulations against drink driving, such as alcohol sales regulations with minimum age limits and maximum levels of blood alcohol concentration (BAC), is key to reducing road accident casualties. For example, higher minimum age limits for purchasing alcohol (up to 21) are applied in the United States, Japan and Korea, together with some northern European countries for certain beverages. Although most countries enforce a BAC level of 0.05 or lower, in many cases countries set lower limits for professional and young drivers. However, broader policy approaches may be required to complement those solely aimed at heavy drinkers. Raising alcohol prices can improve population health through taxes, and doing so in the cheaper segment of the market may be more effective in tackling harmful drinking. In this respect, alcohol taxes are high in northern European countries, Australia and the United Kingdom. Regulating the promotion of alcoholic beverages – such as alcohol advertising, sponsorships and product placement – may provide additional benefits (Sassi, 2015).

OECD analyses show that effective prevention strategies are multifaceted and comprehensive, including both population-wide measures and measures for high-risk individuals. Using all available tools working in unison can strengthen their effectiveness. Such tools include regulation terms of advertising restriction and food labelling; education; incentives such as fiscal measures; health care programmes and services including work site and school interventions; and primary care counselling. Strong advocacy and stakeholder engagement is also needed to develop support for making healthy life style choices easier and less costly. Combining these single interventions in comprehensive strategies results in a more effective and efficient approach because it increases the coverage of groups at risk and exploits potential synergies across the different interventions (OECD, 2010; Sassi, 2015).

Box 3.4. Effective public health interventions across OECD countries *(cont.)*

OECD countries have been implementing policy measures to promote healthy life styles. For example, these days, Denmark, Finland, France, Hungary and Latvia have taken further actions to fight against obesity through the introduction of taxes on unhealthy food and/or sugar-sweetened non-alcoholic beverages. Switzerland, the United Kingdom and the United States introduced nationally co-ordinated health promotion programmes to increase physical activity (OECD, 2015a).

Quality indicators linked to financial incentives aim to improve the quality of primary care

In common with many OECD countries, Latvia has experimented with ways to provide incentives for GPs to improve the quality of the care they deliver to patients. In 2010, a combination of voluntary and compulsory quality incentive systems were introduced for GPs. This comprised a compulsory system with criteria GPs had to achieve to receive their full reimbursement, and a voluntary pay-for-performance system to give GPs incentives to increase quality, particularly in disease prevention and health promotion (Taube et al., 2014). However, only 8.6% of all GPs participated in the voluntary scheme in 2012 because the quality criteria were difficult to achieve, and the financial reward was modest. No GP completed the criteria in 2011, and no GP received payments in 2012 (Mitenbergs et al., 2012).

Latvia tried again with a compulsory scheme introduced in 2013, consisting of 13 criteria. GPs must meet individual annual targets in the domains of prevention, treatment of patients with a chronic condition, increased cost efficiency of health care services, and the diversity of procedures and other services GPs provide (Table 3.1). The indicators mainly relate to the process of care, rather than patient outcomes. In this, once GPs have grown accustomed to the existing performance framework, there is scope to expand it to take in more indicators related to clinical practice and patient outcomes.

Quality bonuses are calculated based on the assessment criteria. GPs are entitled to the full annual quality bonus if they reach or surpass the maximum value of the assessment criteria. If the indicators are within the criteria's permissible range, the quality bonus is adjusted accordingly. GPs who perform below the permissible range, or who fail to provide indicators, lose the quality bonus.

GPs receive payment for achieved quality criteria in the next year, and the payment is made individually to doctors. The average quality payment issued to family doctors in 2013 was EUR 355, accounting for a very small portion of GPs' total annual income. This suggests that the current system is providing insufficient motivation for GPs to improve quality. This is further demonstrated in the data that show at least half of GPs fulfilled the quality criteria in only five of the 13 indicators (Table 3.1). Notably, about three-quarters of GPs achieved the target for health assessments of newly-registered patients, and paediatric health assessments. Otherwise, there is much room for improvement.

A number of factors might explain the modest results thus far. Latvia is still at an early stage in benchmarking performance, but it should be encouraged to persist with this. In common with other countries, Latvian GPs were initially resistant to performance measurement, perhaps due to the fact that most of them are older and are unaccustomed to such disclosure.

Table 3.1. Annual quality assessment of GPs in Latvia

Quality assurance criteria	Total % of GP practices that fulfilled quality criteria in 2013
At least 90% of newly registered patients had a health assessment within three months of registration with a particular GP	73.3
At least 65% of patients over 18 had a health assessment in the past 12 months	55.2
At least 92% of children under 2 have been vaccinated against diphtheria, tetanus, poliomyelitis, pertussis type B, haemophilus influenzae and hepatitis B	39.2
At least 75% of children aged 2 to 18 had a health assessment in the past 12 months	75.6
At least 36% of patients who received breast and cervical cancer screening notifications underwent screening	30.6
At least 8% of 50 to 74-year-old patients had the faecal occult blood test in the past year	10.8
At least 80% of patients with diabetes had the Glycohaemoglobin (Glycosylated Hb) test for type 2 diabetes and at least 60% of checked patients had an haemoglobin A1c result below 7.5%	21.0
At least 60% of patients with type 2 diabetes had the Microalbumin test in the past 12 months	26.8
At least 70% of 50 to 65-year-old patients with arterial hypertension have a cardiovascular risk evaluation every year	17.3
At least 80% of patients with arterial hypertension and patients with coronary heart disease had at least one low-density lipoprotein cholesterol test per year	53.9
At least 75% of patients aged under 6 with bronchial asthma have expiratory flow measurements at least once a year	39.3
GPs' actions to reduce the frequency of calls to the Emergency Medical Service (EMS) where hospitalisation was not required	65.1
GP performed at least 30% of procedures available under his/her professional competence in the past year	19.9

Cancer prevention is one area requiring more attention. Of particular concern is the exceptionally low coverage of faecal occult blood (FOB) test, which is used to screen for colorectal cancer among people aged over 50. Given that the threshold that GPs need to meet is only 8% of the target population, and overwhelmingly GPs are not even achieving that low base, this is an area that would benefit from health promotion campaigns educating the public about the need for screening.

Of equal concern is that less than a third of GPs are meeting the criteria for patients to undergo breast and cervical screening. At a population-wide level, as discussed in Section 3.3, the proportion of Latvians screened for breast, cervical and colorectal cancer is very low, raising questions about whether incentives for GPs to be proactive in cancer screening are sufficient. In the case of cervical and breast screening, it is rare for family doctors to perform this function, although GPs must alert patients to have these tests.

The preventive care of patients with chronic disease is also an area where a low proportion of doctors are meeting the quality criteria. In only one of these indicators, concerning patients receiving cholesterol tests, more than half GPs meet the criteria. As earlier discussed, chronic disease will become a bigger issue for Latvia as its population ages. To be equipped to meet this challenge, preventive care will need to play a bigger role, and GPs will need to be given stronger incentives to take on this role.

The Latvian NHS provides feedback to GPs in the form of an individual report related to the performance of their practice against the quality indicators. GPs can exchange this information with other GPs on a voluntary basis. General information on the quality criteria on which GPs are assessed is also available to the public, but not the performance data.

GPs must now make contact with patients who attend emergency departments, but there is still some way to go to improve care co-ordination between GPs and specialists

Latvia introduced an alert system in 2013, to inform GPs by email about patients who have called for emergency medical assistance but have not been hospitalised. The GP is obliged to contact such patients and agree upon the course of treatment to ensure continuity of care. In the system's first few months, some 400 alerts were sent to GPs.

GPs are also usually notified when their patients have been discharged from hospital, although this is less formalised and depends on the relevant hospital and GP. In some municipalities, GPs are not routinely informed of a patient's discharge, as there is no systematic approach to doing this. However, given GPs can be informed of when patients have sought emergency medical assistance, there is no reason why they cannot also be informed of patient discharge. This is a system that Latvia should work on developing, as GPs should take over the responsibility of care once patients are discharged from hospital into the community. When patients are discharged from hospitals, they receive a statement on the cost of treatment covered by the state. Patients submit this statement to their GP, which provides information on tests that were conducted, treatment, and recommendations for further treatment.

However, despite these attempts to improve care co-ordination across the patient pathway, there is recognition in Latvia that the interaction between primary care and secondary care is insufficient. While patient data collected in the Health Information System is available electronically to a patient's GP and also to a patient upon request, there are currently no regulations facilitating the exchange of electronically-stored information between GPs and specialists.

Latvia is attempting to deal with these challenges in its Primary Healthcare Development Plan. Among the plan's objectives is to improve co-operation between GPs, specialists and other health care providers. Part of this is the development of an electronic health system and, when it is fully implemented, it should help improve the exchange of information between providers.

3.3. Performance of primary health care

There is considerable scope to strengthen primary health care in Latvia, particularly when it comes to preventive measures such as cancer screening. High rates of hospital admissions for asthma also point to the need to improve the care of these patients in primary care. More positively, vaccination coverage has improved considerably and is stronger than it is in many OECD countries. However, access to primary care, particularly outside of office hours, remains a challenging policy issue for Latvia.

The proportion of people who undergo regular cancer screening is very low, contributing to late detection of disease and high case fatality rates

Colorectal cancer screening has the potential to detect both pre-cancerous lesions following a colonoscopy, as well as established cancerous lesions. Therefore, both incidence and the stage of tumour at diagnosis are indicative of the performance of the screening programme, as earlier treatment can improve the possibility of survival. As discussed in the previous section, only about one in ten GPs meet the quality criteria for colorectal cancer screening. Only 13.7% of the target population underwent colorectal screening in 2008, the most recent year data are available (Figure 3.1). While this is higher than it is in many other European countries, it stands in contrast to the efforts of countries such as Germany, the Czech Republic and France (OECD, 2014).

Figure 3.1. Colorectal screening in people aged 50-74, 2008 (or nearest year)

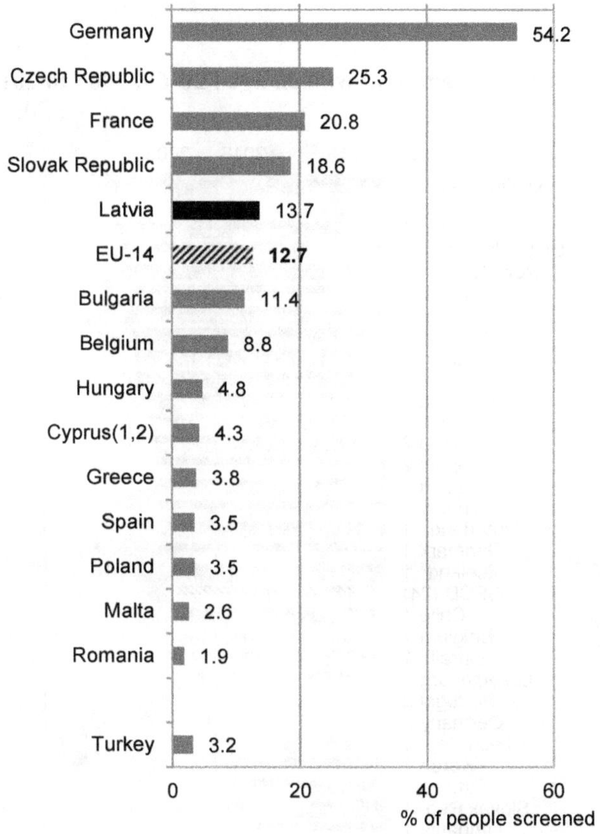

Note: Data based on surveys in all countries.

1. *Note by Turkey:* The information in this report with reference to "Cyprus" relates to the southern part of the Island. There is no single authority representing both Turkish and Greek Cypriot people on the Island. Turkey recognises the Turkish Republic of Northern Cyprus (TRNC). Until a lasting and equitable solution is found within the context of the United Nations, Turkey shall preserve its position concerning the "Cyprus issue".

2. *Note by all the European Union Member States of the OECD and the European Union*: The Republic of Cyprus is recognised by all members of the United Nations with the exception of Turkey. The information in this report relates to the area under the effective control of the Government of the Republic of Cyprus.

Source: Eurostat Statistics Database (based on European Core Health Indicators).

Cervical cancer screening is intended to detect pre-cancerous lesions as well as established cancer, so both the incidence and the stage of detection can be a reflection of the performance of the screening programme. When compared with OECD countries, Latvia has a low rate of screening for cervical cancer, with only 27.4% of the target population screened (OECD, 2015b). By contrast, an average of 61.6% of the target population is screened across the OECD (Figure 3.2). In addition to the organised cervical cancer screening in Latvia, opportunistic screening is still widely applied. The proportion of patients undergoing screening may be higher therefore.

Latvia also fares poorly with regards to breast screening (Figure 3.3), with only 34.2% of women in the target age group undergoing a mammography. This compares with the OECD average of 58.8% (OECD, 2015b). However, unlike colorectal and cervical cancer, mammography can detect only established cancer, so it can have an impact only on the stage at which cancer is detected. Anecdotally, it is understood that some Latvian women are paying to have these tests done themselves, so the rate may be higher. If true, however, this raises the additional question of why women would need, or prefer to, pay for screening.

Figure 3.2. Cervical cancer screening in women aged 20-69, 2003 to 2013 (or nearest year)

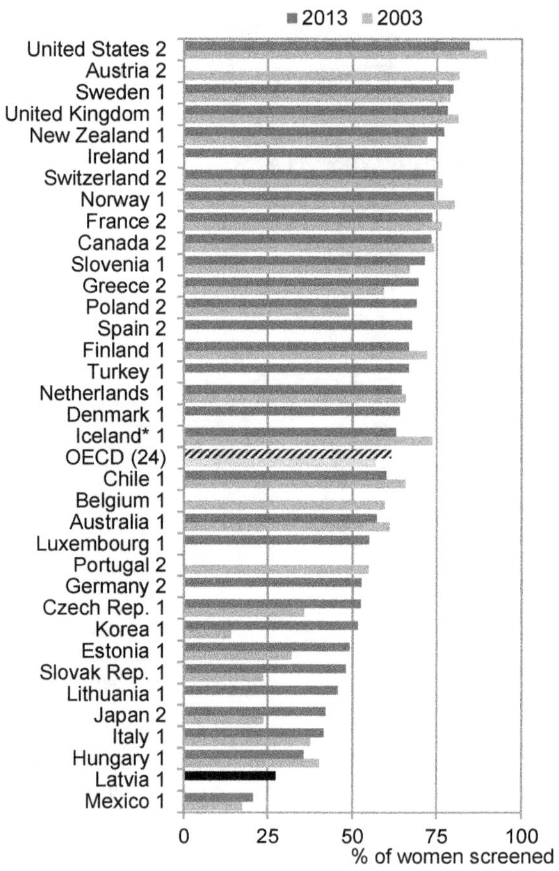

1. Programme.

2. Survey.

* Three-year average.

Source: OECD Health Statistics 2015, http://dx.doi.org/10.1787/health-data-en.

Figure 3.3. Mammography screening in women aged 50-69, 2003 to 2013 (or nearest year)

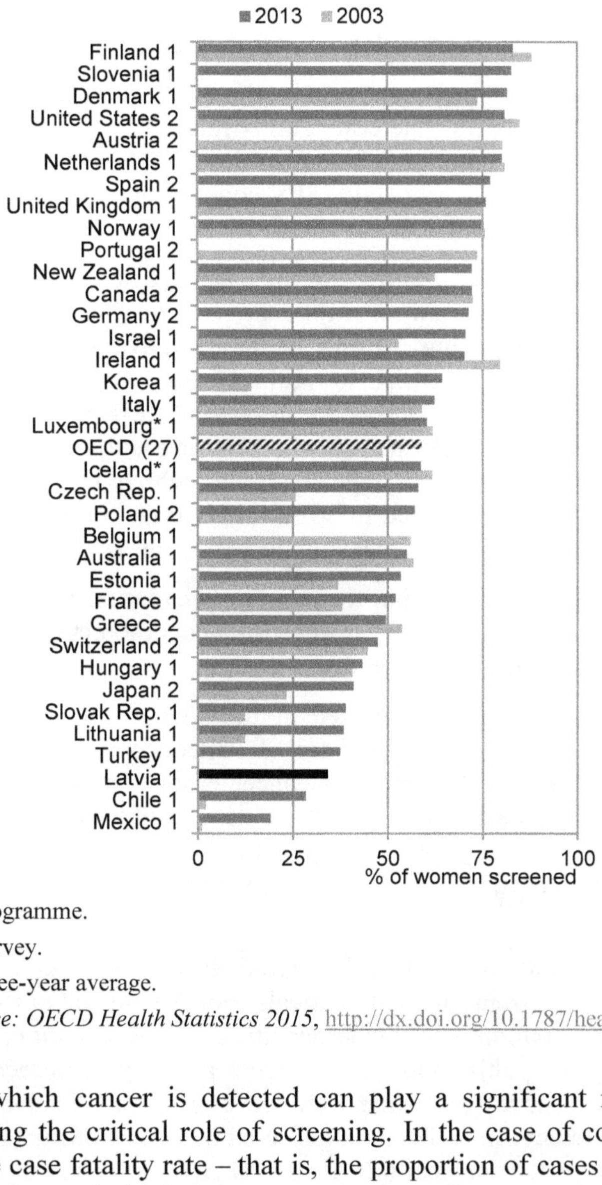

1. Programme.

2. Survey.

* Three-year average.

Source: OECD Health Statistics 2015, http://dx.doi.org/10.1787/health-data-en.

The stage at which cancer is detected can play a significant role in determining survival, highlighting the critical role of screening. In the case of colorectal, breast and cervical cancer, the case fatality rate – that is, the proportion of cases that are fatal within a specified time – is much higher in cases that are diagnosed late at stages 3 and 4 (Table 3.2).

Table 3.2. Cancer stage at diagnosis and case fatality rate

Cancer	Stage at diagnosis (% of cases), 2013					Case fatality rate based on stage of diagnosis, 2012				
	Stage 1	Stage 2	Stage 3	Stage 4	Not known	Stage 1	Stage 2	Stage 3	Stage 4	Not known
Colorectal	12.3	28.8	23.0	23.7	12.2	8.3	14.9	22.6	65.6	63.3
Breast	27.7	36.9	24.6	6.2	4.5	1.7	2.7	11.0	58.9	28.6
Cervical	33.3	13.8	25.3	15.7	11.9	0	14.3	29.5	61.3	40.0

Source: Centre for Disease Prevention and Control (2014), "Register of Patients with Particular Diseases, Patients with Cancer", data updated 24/07/2014.

The significance of this association is evident in the case of colorectal cancer. Very low screening coverage in the country has meant that almost half the cases are diagnosed late at stage 3 or 4. This is concerning, given that two-thirds of cases of colorectal cancer diagnosed at stage 4 and almost a quarter of cases diagnosed at stage 3 are fatal.

The figures are slightly more positive for breast cancer, with two-thirds of cases diagnosed in the first two stages. The case fatality rate for breast cancer demonstrates the life-saving potential of mammography, as fewer than 5% of breast cancer cases are fatal when detected in the first two early stages. By contrast, more than half of breast cancer cases detected at stage 4 are fatal.

Similarly for cervical cancer, almost half the cases are detected in the first two stages. Notably, none of the women diagnosed with cervical cancer at stage 1 died in 2012. The data suggest that better engaging GPs to be more active in encouraging patients to undergo screening has the potential to reduce cancer mortality by increasing the proportion of patients diagnosed early. As discussed earlier in this chapter, GPs can receive payments of EUR 71.14 per patient to detect first and second-stage cancer in their registered patients, but it is unclear the extent to which this has been an effective incentive. This system was introduced in 2013, and Latvian authorities intend to measure its effectiveness. In 2013, 1 152 GPs received this payment, and 1 143 in 2014.

In addition, Latvia has tried to improve cancer prevention with its 2009 launch of a public screening programme for breast, cervical and colorectal cancer. However, the response thus far seems to have been modest.

Latvia has a Cancer Registry, located at the Centre for Disease Prevention and Control (CDPC), and a part of the Register of Patients with Particular Diseases. It is mandatory for all providers to report new cancer cases. The data are used to estimate cancer incidence, prevalence and survival. The data are published on the CDPC's website (http://www.spkc.gov.lv/veselibas-aprupes-statistika/) and have also been used for planning and evaluation of health services (International Association of Cancer Registries, 2015).

Latvia requires a national population-based system that keeps a record of the screening history of all citizens, and automatically notifies people of their need to undergo screening. Such a programme should be accompanied by a national public awareness campaign, educating the public about the dangers in delaying screening and diagnosis. Education campaigns should particularly be developed for disadvantaged populations with poorer health literacy. In 2013, the NHS conducted an information campaign about cancer screening: "Check your health, the state is paying!" The campaign has not been evaluated so its impact is unknown.

Other indicators of the quality of primary health care present a mixed picture

Hospital admission rates for asthma, chronic obstructive pulmonary disease (COPD) and diabetes can be considered an indirect measure of the quality of primary care for these conditions, as these hospitalisations are potentially preventable if they are well-managed in primary care. Latvia's performance with regards to age-sex standardised hospital admission rates vary when compared with the average across OECD countries (Figures 3.4 and 3.5).

Of particular note is Latvia's high rate of hospital admission for asthma (95.2 per 100 000 population, compared with the OECD average of 43.8 per 100 000 population) (OECD, 2015b). As discussed in the previous section, quite a low proportion of GPs are meeting the prescribed quality criteria for processes related to patient care for chronic disease, and this is particularly the case for asthma. This is where second practice nurses could play a bigger role, and where incentives for GPs could be strengthened.

However, Latvia fares better when it comes to hospital admissions for COPD, with 161.7 per 100 000 population compared with the OECD average of 198.4 per 100 000 population. Latvia's rate of hospital admission for diabetes is also lower than that of the OECD average (131.2 compared with 149.8 per 100 000 population (OECD, 2015b).

Figure 3.4. Asthma and COPD hospital admissions in adults, 2013 (or nearest year)

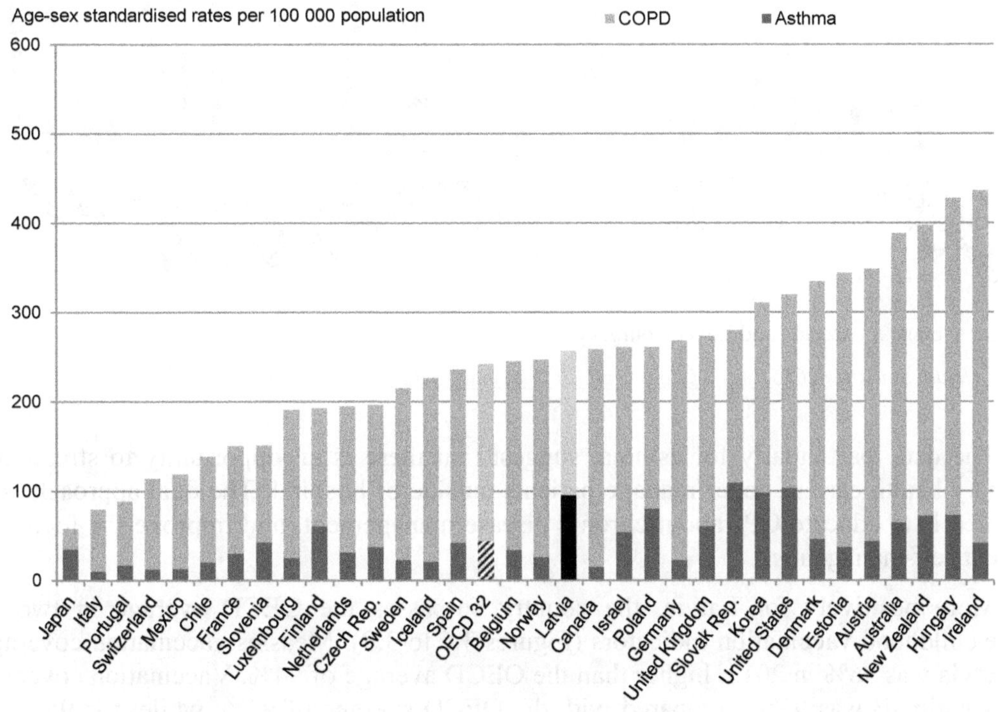

Note: Three-year average for Iceland and Luxembourg. COPD: Chronic obstructive pulmonary disease.

Source: OECD Health Statistics 2015, http://dx.doi.org/10.1787/health-data-en.

Figure 3.5. Diabetes hospital admission in adults, 2008 and 2013 (or nearest year)

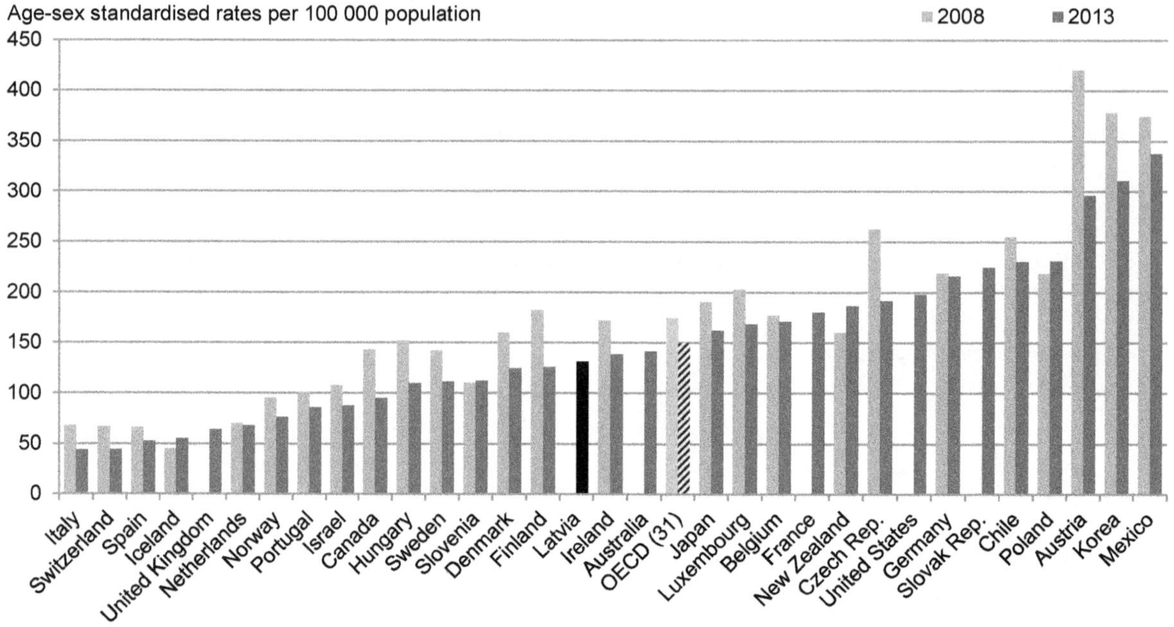

Note: Three-year average for Iceland and Luxembourg.

Source: OECD Health Statistics 2015, http://dx.doi.org/10.1787/health-data-en.

The data, particularly for asthma, suggest that there is an opportunity to strengthen primary health care to better manage patients outside of hospital. The dual approach best adopted is to educate GPs about chronic disease management, and improve the focus on patient self-management.

More positively for Latvia, the country surpasses the OECD average in two of three childhood vaccination indicators (Figures 3.6 to 3.8). Measles vaccination coverage in Latvia was 96% in 2013, higher than the OECD average of 94%. Vaccination coverage for hepatitis B was 95%, compared with the OECD average of 92%, while it is 95% for diphtheria, tetanus and pertussis, the same as the OECD average (OECD, 2015b).

Figure 3.6. Vaccination against diphteria, tetanus and pertussis, children aged 1, 2013

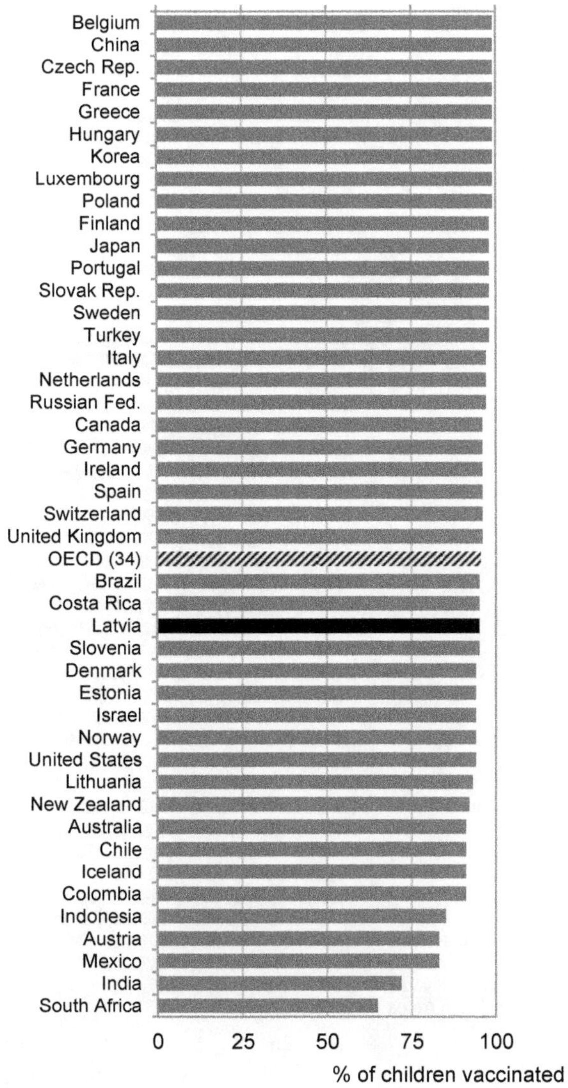

Source: WHO/UNICEF.

Figure 3.7. Vaccination against measles, children aged 1, 2013

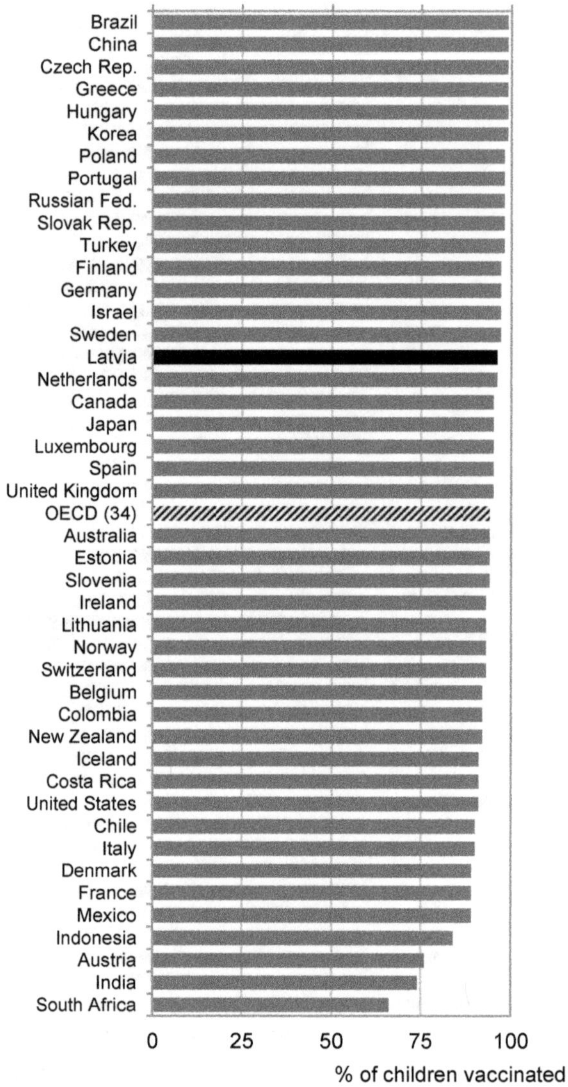

Source: WHO/UNICEF.

Figure 3.8. Vaccination against hepatitis B, children aged 1, 2013

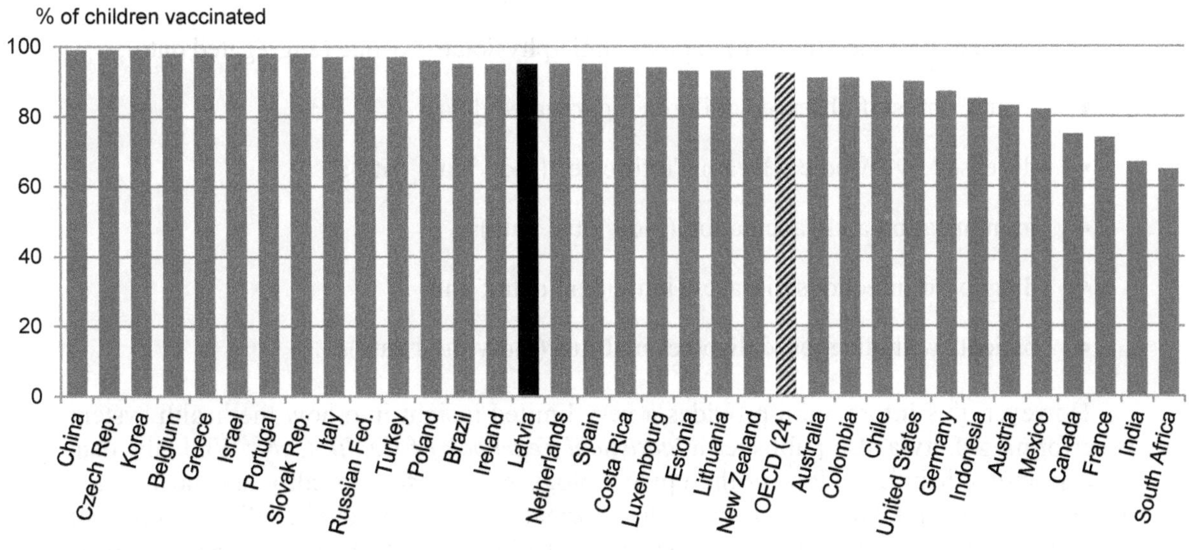

Source: WHO/UNICEF.

Coverage in Latvia had fallen after 2008, and was below the World Health Organization's target of 95%. This was explained by socioeconomic factors, and an increase in vaccination opponents (Taube et al., 2014).

Latvia's progress in lifting these rates above 95% could be explained by concerted efforts in the form of Regulations on Vaccination and the Immunisation Plan for 2012-14 and establishing state-funded planned vaccination against a range of vaccine-preventable infectious diseases (CDPC, 2013). To continue these efforts, Public Health Guidelines for 2014-20 include concrete measures in the field of prophylaxis of infectious diseases and vaccination policy. The Centre for Disease Prevention and Control prepares motivating campaigns and brochures promoting vaccination and information regarding infectious diseases. In 2015, the Centre conducted a study to understand the reasons parents refuse vaccination of their children. The results of this study are being analysed and will be used to help conduct more targeted vaccination campaigns.

Not enough is known about quality and outcomes in primary health care

The publication of data informing people of the quality and outcomes of their health system is a critical component of patient-centred care. Yet there is little information giving Latvian citizens an indication of how well their primary health care system is performing, particularly comparative information that can help inform decisions people make about providers.

The previous section discussed the data GPs are required to provide as part of the pay-for-performance scheme. This includes the proportion of patients who have a health assessment, cancer screening notifications, and indicators related to chronic disease. However, these are largely indicators about the process of care, and reveal nothing about patients' clinical outcomes.

It is mandatory for GPs to report the following information to public authorities:

- employees in the institution (aggregated data);
- services provided in the outpatient clinic/physician's office (aggregated data);
- health status of observed children (aggregated data);
- deceased by "Medical Death Certificate" (individual data);
- immunisation and vaccination (individual data);
- diagnosed infectious diseases (individual data); and
- patients with diagnosed diabetes mellitus (individual data).

However, this information provides a very limited insight into how the health system is performing. Latvia also publishes a *Statistical Yearbook of Health Care.* While the data provide in-depth information on the epidemiology of disease, mortality and health care resources and hospital activity, there is no information on health care quality, and patient outcomes. For example, little is known about patient safety in primary care, such as adverse events. Nor is there information collected about patient experience in ambulatory care, and there is no requirement for general practices to collect information about the work of nurses or physician assistants – despite the vital role they play in delivering primary care services.

Latvia has acknowledged these information deficits in its Primary Health Care Development Plan, and is working towards improving the availability of information to the public. Countries that have developed comprehensive quality indicators include Israel and the United Kingdom, which have both adopted extensive frameworks to measure primary care performance (Box 3.5).

Box 3.5. Measuring primary care performance

In Israel, health funds have a sophisticated information infrastructure that supports care delivery and quality monitoring. The Quality Indicators in Community Healthcare (QIHC) programme involves the systematic collection of data for the entire population of Israel from all four health plans to create national-level quality indicators that are publically reported (Jaffe et al., 2012).

The QICH indicators cover six clinical areas: asthma, breast and colorectal cancer screening, immunisation for older people, child and adolescent health, cardiovascular health, and diabetes. The focus on prevention is demonstrated by the inclusion of indicators relating to risk factors, such as BMI. The programme is not compulsory, but its success is due to the voluntary involvement of the health funds in its conception and design, their active participation in developing the indicators, and the consensus around a scientifically robust quality measurement programme (OECD, 2012).

There is evidence that the programme has improved quality. One evaluation found documentation of BMI for adolescents and adults increased by 30 percentage points to 61% and 70% respectively. Other improvements were an increase in the appropriate use of asthma control medication, while the rates of influenza vaccination among Israelis aged 65 and over increased from 52% to 57%. The authors concluded the overall quality of community health care in Israel had improved in the previous three years (Jaffe et al., 2012). While physicians in Israel do not receive financial incentives for participating in the programme, it could be argued that they benefit from the feedback they receive, which enables them to compare their performance to that of their peers. This can provide a persuasive incentive for doctors to improve quality of care.

Box 3.5. Measuring primary care performance *(cont.)*

The United Kingdom's voluntary Quality and Outcomes Framework (QOF) takes this further by linking performance to financial incentives. Payments from QOF can constitute as much as a third of a general practice's income (Willcox et al., 2011). QOF comprises almost 150 indicators covering chronic disease management and other areas. Each indicator is weighted, and general practices accumulate points that are used to determine the payments they receive. The performance of every practice is publicly reported on a website.

Some of the indicators include the establishment of disease registers. For example, one register relates to the percentage of patients aged 14 to 19 with asthma for whom there is a record of smoking status. QOF also has a stronger focus on clinical outcomes. For instance, one indicator relates to the percentage of patients on the chronic kidney disease register whose notes include a record of blood pressure, while another indicator links that to patient outcomes in that the blood pressure measure is 140/85 or less. There are also ten indicators related to mental health, such as the percentage of women with schizophrenia, bipolar affective disorder and other psychoses who have had a cervical screening test.

While the existence of more than 100 indicators may not necessarily be useful or drive quality gains, the QOF scheme demonstrates that there is significant scope to introduce a more comprehensive primary care performance framework, and link it to quality patient care.

Source: OECD (2015), *OECD Reviews of Health Care Quality: Australia 2015: Raising Standards*, OECD Publishing, Paris, http://dx.doi.org/10.1787/9789264233836-en.

Access to primary care is also limited, especially outside of office hours

The Latvian Primary Health Care Development Plan acknowledges that access to a GP can be challenging and patients cannot always get an appointment in a five-day work period. The plan cites FINBALT research data showing that 12.3% of survey respondents who visited a GP in the previous year waited for a doctor for more than one week.

In common with many OECD countries, access to primary care is most challenging outside of office hours. Latvia's GPs are not obliged to provide practice work in the evenings after 7pm, or on weekends.

The dominant mode of providing out-of-hours (OOH) primary care in Latvia in both urban and rural areas is companies employing doctors to take over the provision of OOH care. In urban areas, on-call doctors see patients on evenings and weekends and holidays in accordance with the work schedule included in the NHS contract. The on-call doctor attends to all residents in their catchment area, regardless of which family doctor the patient is registered with. All medical treatment facilities must display information about the office hours of each GP, and how to see the on-call doctor.

On-call doctors also perform home visits for particular groups, including children, patients over 80 and people with particular disabilities. They are provided in the largest cities, with one on-call doctor for every 40 000 patients. This equates to about 26 on-call doctors in Latvia. An extension to OOH care in the country is a family doctor advice hotline that operates from 5pm to 8am on weekdays, and 24 hours on weekends and holidays. Family doctors and physician assistants provide medical advice about simple illnesses. Patients can contact the hotline by telephone, e-mail or Skype. Since its launch in 2011, the hotline has been contacted by on average 5 597 patients per month. This service is free for patients, who pay only the cost of an ordinary phone call.

Despite these initiatives, there is recognition in Latvia that the current means of providing OOH primary care is not sufficient. Many countries are grappling with the problem of so-called "inappropriate" use of hospital emergency departments by patients who cannot access a GP on evenings and weekends. In Latvia, OOH GP access ends at 10pm, and after this, patients have to go to an emergency department.

The need to improve the provision of OOH care has received intense policy attention from many OECD countries. An effective OOH primary care system is one that improves the experience for patients by providing timely and high-quality care, reduces the burden on physicians, and negates the need for more costly unnecessary hospital care. Some countries, such as The Netherlands and Denmark, have found large-scale general practice co-operatives to be an effective policy lever (Box 3.6).

Box 3.6. General Practice Cooperatives in the Netherlands

General Practice Cooperatives (GPCs) are large-scale organisations of primary care physicians providing OOH care. Participation is mandatory for GPs, who take turns on a roster basis to be on OOH duty for all the patients of all the participating GPs in a specified region. Given all GPs participate, the burden is significantly reduced.

Nurses perform telephone triage, supervised by GPs. This is usually the first point of contact for patients, although a small proportion of patients attend the clinic without calling in advance. GPs also perform house calls when deemed necessary. Electronic health records are used to promote continuity of patient care between providers.

Since the GPCs began taking shape in 2000, they have undergone several evaluations. Studies have demonstrated that patient satisfaction with GPCs is high. GPCs have reduced the workload of doctors and increased their satisfaction. This is an important development, as reluctance of GPs to provide OOH care due to the workload burden is often a major barrier.

Studies have also found that GPCs can help reduce health system costs by shifting care from the emergency department to primary care.

Source: Giesen et al. (2011); Smits et al. (2012); Van Uden et al. (2005); Van Uden et al. (2006); Van Uden and Crebolder (2004).

3.4. Strengthening primary health care in Latvia

Latvia has a good base of policies, institutions, financial and informational frameworks in place to underpin delivery of effective primary care. Several steps should be taken, however, to strengthen the sector and, in particular, improve how chronic disease is prevented and treated. There is scope to improve access to primary care services, in the short term by developing nurses' and pharmacists' roles, focussed on improving how chronic disease is prevented and treated. A key priority must be to collect and publish more information on the quality and outcomes achieved by primary care, and use performance-based incentives to drive continuous improvement. Continued innovation in the models of care, especially in how primary care and secondary care are integrated, is also needed.

Access to primary care should be improved by expanding professional roles

Given the increasingly prominent role that primary care is expected play in Latvia, the problems with access referred to earlier need to be addressed. In the longer term, the number of training and residency places should be expanded. Expansion is underway, but has thus far has been modest (from 22 training places in 2012, to 28 in 2014). An acceleration of training capacity should be considered, informed by modelling of future workforce needs and building on Latvia's strong tradition of world-class medical education. The issue is urgent, given that more than a quarter of GPs are older than 60 and hence about to retire.

In the shorter term, the roles of other primary care professionals should be better developed to support the work of GPs. Latvia has already innovated in this regard, by funding second practice nurses and physician assistants. It appears, however, that potential contribution of these professional groups is not yet fully realised. Second nurses, for example, rarely assist in co-ordinating the care of patients with chronic conditions.

Across the OECD, nurses with additional specialist training are undertaking an increasingly wide range of primary care tasks, particularly around chronic disease management. A number of systematic reviews comparing nurse practitioners and physicians working in primary care have shown that the performance and outcomes of nurse practitioners equals and in some cases exceeds that of physicians, with nurses often scoring higher on patient satisfaction, communication, and giving advice and patient support (Horrocks et al., 2002; Newhouse et al., 2011; Health Affairs, 2013).

The range of tasks performed by nurse practitioners varies between countries. In Sweden, nurse-led clinics provide for patients with long-term conditions, such as diabetes and heart failure as in Sweden, and nurses play a role in co-ordinating care for chronically ill patients. In Denmark, nurses have taken on new roles managing elderly patients and others with complex, chronic care needs, particularly in the context of services provided. In England nurse practitioners increasingly run their own specialist clinics, including clinical assessment, ordering investigations, referring for onward care, clinical management and, in some settings, prescribing for specific clinical situations.

Community pharmacists offer another potential development and Latvia starts from a strong position here, given that pharmacists already offer consultations regarding medicines use, and some aspects of health promotion and disease prevention. Nevertheless, there is scope to look at leading-edge practice elsewhere and develop pharmacists' role further. In Norway, for example, pharmacists commonly offer cardiovascular health checks in a programme welcomed by the Norwegian Diabetes Association and other patient groups.

Professional associations and policy makers in Latvia should study international experience, and consider how nurses' and pharmacists' roles should be further developed locally to reflect international trends. Given rather unique history of *feldshers* in Latvia, the country has the potential to be internationally innovative in how the primary care workforce is composed. A rich information infrastructure, describing the activities, costs and outcomes achieved by a diversified and expanded Latvian primary care workforce would have substantial international value.

Prevention and treatment of long-term conditions can be improved by further developing incentives, with a clearer focus on outcomes

There is strong recognition in Latvia of the need for a renewed focus on preventive health care and management long-term conditions at national level. In terms of primary prevention, through health promotion and public health activities, Latvia has already implemented several nation-wide initiatives. More needs to be done, however, with secondary prevention – that is, the management of already established risk factors such as obesity or high blood pressure, and screening.

Latvia's *Annual Quality Assessment* of GPs is a promising attempt to quantify and improve the impact of primary care on secondary prevention and screening (it also includes primary prevention activities). In 2013, however, the numbers of GPs reaching the specified thresholds for screening and secondary prevention was relatively modest – for most indicators, less than half of GPs were successful (Table 3.1). This is despite the fact that the thresholds were not overly ambitious (for example, that at least 36% of patients receiving notification for breast and cervical cancer screening underwent screening). In addition, all thresholds relate to process measures, which are generally easier to achieve than thresholds linked to clinical outcomes. Disappointing performance to date may be because the programme needs more time to mature, and/or that the incentives contained within the programme are not strong enough. Certainly, the financial incentive does not appear substantial: the average payment in 2013 was EUR 355.

It is too soon to abandon the *Annual Quality Assessment* scheme, and its evolving impact on practice should be closely observed. There may be structural factors (such as a lack of workforce, or poor IT systems) that are holding back performance, and that will not improve over time without additional investment. An active programme of audit and research should be encouraged, with a focus on transparent comparison of providers' results. Clinicians and academics should be encouraged to lead this work, with government authorities taking strategic oversight – particularly to ensure that findings lead to service improvement, nationally and locally. Variation within Latvia should be studied closely, both as a means to improve performance overall as well as tackle inequalities. Comparing the performance of Latvian GPs against international peers (through the *OECD Health Care Quality Indicators* programme which benchmarks, amongst other things, appropriate prescribing for patients with diabetes) will be an important signal of the system's maturity.

Proactive investigation is also needed to understand some unexplained phenomena, such as the anecdotal observation that breast and cervical cancer screening rates appear low because women are paying to have these tests done themselves. It is unclear why women would need, or prefer to, pay for screening if available for free from their GP.

At the same time, the experiences of successful primary care incentive schemes internationally should be studied to inform on-going evolution of Latvia's *Annual Quality Assessment* scheme. Israel's *Quality Indicators in Community Healthcare* (QICH) programme is well-established, and distinctive because it has driven significant quality improvements purely on the basis of peer-to-peer benchmarking, without financial incentives. A number of clinical outcomes (such as successful control of blood pressure, cholesterol and glycaemia in diabetics) are included to complement process measures (OECD, 2012). The benchmarks published by the QICH are intended for patients' information and use, as much as doctors' or managers'. Hence it may be that greater public awareness of GPs' performance in Latvia's *Annual Quality Assessment* scheme will be an important tool to step up improvements.

Other primary care systems have used financial incentives alongside peer-to-peer benchmarking. The United Kingdom's Quality and Outcomes Framework (QOF) is particularly sophisticated and financially incentivises GPs against process measures (monitoring, prescribing and counselling); intermediate clinical outcomes (glycated hemoglobin, cholesterol and blood pressure); and patient-reported indicators, such as quality of life and satisfaction with care (OECD, 2016). The approach taken in Australia is also instructive. There, the Practice Incentives Programme (PIP) has three components – the sign-on payment, outcomes payment and service incentive payment for patients with diabetes. The sign-on payment is a one-off payment to practices that use a patient register and recall and reminder system for their patients with diabetes mellitus. The second component (outcomes payments) is triggered if at least 2% of practice patients are diagnosed with diabetes mellitus, and GPs have completed a cycle of care for at least 50% of these patients. The cycle of care includes measurement of HbA1c, foot and eye examination; weight and height; measurement of blood pressure and cholesterol and health promotion. The third component is an additional payment each independent cycle of care completed for patients with established diabetes mellitus (OECD, 2015c).

Better integration with hospital services can be achieved through innovative service models

Latvia has acknowledged the need to develop a more patient-centred, integrated health system that makes greater use of primary care and relies less on expensive hospital care (as articulated, for example, in the Primary Health Care Development Plan, Box 3.3). Better integration with emergency services has been helped by the new requirement that GPs contact patients who have called for emergency medical assistance but have not been hospitalised, and broader integration with essential public services beyond the health system was also intended through the Social Safety Net Strategy and new models of co-operation between GPs and home care providers.

Closer integration with other parts of the health system is needed, however. Although Latvia has innovated in professional roles, service models remain highly traditional – a substantial disconnect still characterises relations between primary and secondary care. This is evidenced by the lack of systematic mechanisms to ensure that patients are followed up in the community after discharge from a planned hospital care, and lack of regulations to facilitate the exchange of electronically-stored information between GPs and specialists. Additional mechanisms are needed to allow GPs to stay involved across a patient's entire pathway of care, a particularly important issue given increasing prevalence of patients with multiple, complex needs.

An important international innovation in the service model, that Latvia appears to have not yet explored, concerns diseases management programmes. These create new multi-professional networks to provide an integrated package of care for specified patient groups. Disease management programmes are particularly well developed in Germany. They enrol patients with diabetes or other chronic diseases at an early stage, and place an emphasis on care co-ordination, secondary prevention and the use of evidence-based guidelines. To be eligible for the programme, patients must be willing to participate in managing their own disease. A number of innovations in England (Box 3.7), concerning regulation and funding flows, also serve as illustrations for Latvia to consider.

Box 3.7. Improving patient-centred, integrated care in England

In England's publicly-funded, single-payer system, health care services are planned and purchased by local clinical commissioning groups (CCGs). CCGs are subject to an assurance framework which attempts to prioritise patient-centred, integrated care. The framework uses a set of delivery metrics focussed on aspects such as digital record keeping and transfers of care, with particular attention to five population groups: the generally well, people with long-term conditions, people with mental health problems or learning disabilities, children and young people, and the frail elderly.

Promoting integration is one of the broad objectives of Commissioning for Quality and Innovation (CQUIN) payment framework. CQUIN allows CCGs to incentivise better care by linking a proportion of health care providers' income to agreed quality goals. The 2015/16 scheme is structured so that the goals reward transformation across care pathways that cut across different providers.

The independent regular of health and social care services (the Care Quality Commission) is also undertaking cross-cutting reviews of care for particular patient groups, such as the elderly. These are intended to assess and improve quality in community services and across transitions of care.

Personal health budgets are a powerful idea to drive better co-ordination and integration from the bottom-up. They aim to give people with long-term conditions and disabilities greater control over the care they receive by giving individuals a sum of money to spend on services or equipment, agreed between themselves and their professional careers.

References

CDPC – Centre for Disease Prevention and Control (2014), *Statistical Yearbook of Health Care in Latvia 2013*, Riga.

CDPC (2013), *Health of the Population of Latvia, 2002-2012*.

Eurostat (2015a), "Physicians by Medical Speciality", last update 14/08/2015, available at: http://appsso.eurostat.ec.europa.eu/nui/submitViewTableAction.do (accessed 01/10/2015).

Eurostat (2015b), "Self-reported Unmet Needs for Medical Examination by Sex, age, Detailed Reason and Educational Attainment Level", last update 26/03/2015, available at: http://appsso.eurostat.ec.europa.eu/nui/submitViewTableAction.do (accessed 20/10/2015).

Giesen, P. et al (2011), "Quality of After-hours Primary Care in the Netherlands: A Narrative Review", *Annals of Internal Medicine*, Vol. 155, No. 2, pp. 108-113, http://dx.doi.org/10.7326/0003-4819-155-2-201107190-00006.

International Association of Cancer Registries (2015), *Latvian Cancer Registry Profile Page,* available at: http://www.iacr.com.fr/index.php?option=com_comprofiler&task=userprofile&user=1048&Itemid=498 (accessed 16/10/2015).

Jaffe, D.H. et al (2012), "Community Healthcare in Israel: Quality Indicators 2007-2009", *Israel Journal of Health Policy Research*, Vol. 1, No. 1, p. 3, http://dx.doi.org/10.1186/2045-4015-1-3.

Mitenbergs, U. et al (2012), "Latvia: Health System Review", *Health Systems in Transition*, Vol. 14, No. 8, pp. 1-191.

OECD (2016), *OECD Reviews of Health Care Quality: United Kingdom 2016: Raising Standards*, OECD Publishing, Paris. http://dx.doi.org/10.1787/9789264239487-en.

OECD (2015a), *Cardiovascular Disease and Diabetes: Policies for Better Health and Quality of Care*, OECD Health Policy Studies, OECD Publishing, Paris, http://dx.doi.org/10.1787/9789264233010-en.

OECD (2015b), *Health at a Glance 2015: OECD Indicators*, OECD Publishing, Paris, http://dx.doi.org/10.1787/health_glance-2015-en.

OECD (2015c), *OECD Reviews of Health Care Quality: Australia 2015: Raising Standards*, OECD Publishing, Paris, http://dx.doi.org/10.1787/9789264233836-en.

OECD (2015d), *OECD Reviews of Health Care Quality: Portugal 2015: Raising Standards*, OECD Publishing, Paris. http://dx.doi.org/10.1787/9789264225985-en.

OECD (2014), *Health at a Glance Europe 2014,* OECD Publishing, Paris, http://dx.doi.org/10.1787/health_glance_eur-2014-en.

OECD (2012), "Strengthening Community-based Primary Health Care", *OECD Reviews of Health Care Quality: Israel 2012: Raising Standards*, OECD Publishing, Paris, http://dx.doi.org/10.1787/9789264029941-6-en.

OECD (2010), *Obesity and the Economics of Prevention: Fit not Fat*, OECD Publishing, Paris, http://dx.doi.org/10.1787/9789264084865-en.

Sassi, F. (ed.) (2015), *Tackling Harmful Alcohol Use: Economics and Public Health Policy*, OECD Publishing, Paris, http://dx.doi.org/10.1787/9789264181069-en.

Smits, M. et al (2012), "Patient Satisfaction with Out-of-hours GP Cooperatives: A Longitudinal Study", *Scandinavian Journal of Primary Health Care*, Vol. 30, No. 4, pp. 206-213, http://dx.doi.org/10.3109/02813432.2012.735553.

Taube, M., U. Mitenbergs and A. Sagan (2014), *The Impact of the Financial Crisis on the Health System and Health in Latvia*, European Observatory on Health Systems and Policies, World Health Organization.

Van Uden, C.J.T. and H.F.J.M. Crebolder (2004), "Does Setting Up Out of Hours Primary Care Cooperatives Outside a Hospital Reduce Demand for Emergency Care?", *Emergency Medicine Journal*, Vol. 21, No. 6, pp. 722-723, http://dx.doi.org/10.1136/emj.2004.016071.

Van Uden, C.J.T. et al (2006), "Development of Out-of-hours Primary Care by General Practitioners (GPs) in the Netherlands: From Small-call Rotations to Large-scale GP Cooperatives", *International Family Medicine*, Vol. 38, No. 8, pp. 565-569.

Van Uden, C.J.T. et al (2005), "Patient Satisfaction with Out-of-hours Primary Care in the Netherlands", *BMC Health Services Research*, Vol. 5, No. 1, p. 6, http://dx.doi.org/10.1186/1472-6963-5-6.

Willcox, S., G. Lewis and J. Burgers (2011), "Strengthening Primary Care: Recent Reforms and Achievements in Australia, England and the Netherlands", *Issues in International Health Policy*, The Commonwealth Fund, Pub. 1564, Vol. 27.

World Bank (2015), "The Active Aging Challenge for Longer Working Lives in Latvia", http://pubdocs.worldbank.org/en/205791443642635843/WB-Latvia-Active-Aging-Report.pdf.

ORGANISATION FOR ECONOMIC CO-OPERATION AND DEVELOPMENT

The OECD is a unique forum where governments work together to address the economic, social and environmental challenges of globalisation. The OECD is also at the forefront of efforts to understand and to help governments respond to new developments and concerns, such as corporate governance, the information economy and the challenges of an ageing population. The Organisation provides a setting where governments can compare policy experiences, seek answers to common problems, identify good practice and work to co-ordinate domestic and international policies.

The OECD member countries are: Australia, Austria, Belgium, Canada, Chile, the Czech Republic, Denmark, Estonia, Finland, France, Germany, Greece, Hungary, Iceland, Ireland, Israel, Italy, Japan, Korea, Latvia, Luxembourg, Mexico, the Netherlands, New Zealand, Norway, Poland, Portugal, the Slovak Republic, Slovenia, Spain, Sweden, Switzerland, Turkey, the United Kingdom and the United States. The European Union takes part in the work of the OECD.

OECD Publishing disseminates widely the results of the Organisation's statistics gathering and research on economic, social and environmental issues, as well as the conventions, guidelines and standards agreed by its members.

OECD PUBLISHING, 2, rue André-Pascal, 75775 PARIS CEDEX 16
(81 2016 14 1 P) ISBN 978-92-64-26276-8 – 2016

www.ingramcontent.com/pod-product-compliance
Lightning Source LLC
Chambersburg PA
CBHW061219240926
51846CB00006B/1283
* 9 7 8 9 2 6 4 2 6 2 7 6 8 *